EXPLORING THE
ATTRIBUTES OF GOD

EXPLORING THE ATTRIBUTES OF GOD

*An Apologetic for the Biblical
Doctrine of God*

DR. ROBERT A. MOREY

WORLD
BIBLE PUBLISHERS, INC.
Iowa Falls, IA 50126 U.S.A.

World Bible Publishers, Inc.
Iowa Falls, IA 50126

Printed in the United States of America.

ISBN 0-529-11372-4

1   2   3   4   5   BGP   05   04   03   02   01

ABOUT THE AUTHOR

*D*r. Bob Morey, Executive Director of the Research and Education Foundation, is the author of over forty books, some of which have been translated into French, German, Italian, Polish, Finish, Dutch, Spanish, Norwegian, Swedish, and Chinese. He has doctorates in apologetics and Islamic studies. For more information on his ministry, write to:

> Faith Defenders
> P.O. Box 7447
> Orange, CA 92863
>
> www.faithdefenders.com.
> 1-800-41-TRUTH.

Other books by Dr. Morey:
> *Fearing God*
> *The Trinity: Evidence and Issues*
> *Satan's Devices*
> *The Islamic Invasion*
> *The Truth about Masons*
> *Death and the Afterlife*
> *Studies in the Atonement*
> *Battle of the Gods*
> *The New Atheism and the Erosion of Freedom*
> *An Introduction to Defending the Faith*
> *How to Keep Your Faith While in College*
> *An Analysis of the Hadith*
> *When Is It Right to Fight?*

To Bruce and Mary
faithful servants
of the King

CONTENTS

INTRODUCTION

"Here Is Your God!"

T he Scriptures are abundantly clear that the knowledge of God is the goal of salvation (John 17:3) and the Christian life (Philemon 3:8-10). Indeed, the failure to know God will be the basis of divine judgment when Christ returns in glory (II Thessalonians 1:7-8). Thus if we fail in our lifetime to come to a saving knowledge of the one true God who has revealed Himself in Scripture, we will forever be cut off from that knowledge.

Knowing God comes in two phases. First, there must an intellectual knowledge of God. Jesus demanded that we must have TRUE ideas and concepts of Who and What God is like in His divine nature (John 4:24). Thus God calls upon us to use our minds as we worship Him (Matthew 22:37). Our minds are to renewed and transformed by His power (Romans 12:2). We must not be "mindless" or irrational when it comes to the knowledge of God.

Second, we must go beyond a mere intellectual grasp of the biblical nature of God and actually encounter the living God by personally placing our faith and hope in Him. Thus true saving faith involves three things:

1. An intellectual understanding of the God revealed in Scripture.
2. An agreement and approval that the biblical view of God is true.

1

3. A personal commitment to God in which you choose to
    worship and serve only Him.

Any "knowledge" of God that fails to begin in the mind and end
in the heart is like a bridge broken at either end. We cannot personally
know God until we intellectually know about God.

Do you know what God is like? Can you define His attributes and
explain His nature? What makes God GOD? Are you believing in the
right God? Or, have you been worshipping a false God?

These questions are answered in this study guide on the attributes
of God. The goal of this study is to bring you into a deeper understanding and appreciation of the God who has revealed Himself in Scripture.

> To Him be all the glory,
> forever and ever, Amen.

ONE

RELIGION, REASON, AND REVELATION

The main problem we face today when discussing the nature of God is that people are not willing to limit their beliefs to what the Bible clearly teaches. Throughout the present controversy over the omniscience of God one searches in vain to find a single finite god advocate who bothers to give any serious exegesis of Scripture. Why is this?

Instead of a careful exegesis of Scripture, "evangelical" processians and "moral government" teachers appeal to "reason," "intuition," and "experience" as all the proof they need. Thus they never bother to let the Bible decide such issues because their doctrines are chosen on the basis of what feels "comfortable" or sounds "reasonable" to them. Doctrinal truth is often decided on the basis of how it will supposedly affect prayer, evangelism, or missions.

Among liberals and neo-evangelicals, the Bible is ignored for the most part because it is assumed that the Scriptures do not contain any propositional revelation and hence cannot be used for theology. It is claimed that the Bible is not the Word of God but that it "becomes the Word of God" when it speaks to us, or that revelation is limited to a nonrational personal encounter with God who is identified as "unknown X."

The Christian Church has always taught that the God who created man in His image has no difficulty in communicating truth to man. God reveals in Scripture true propositions about Himself, and also personally confronts man in grace or judgment.

The liberal bias against the Bible is based on a humanistic either/or dichotomy. It is assumed that either God reveals only Himself or else He reveals only facts about Himself, but not both. Such men refuse to

3

consider the rather obvious alternative that God's revelation is both personal and factual. Not only is the Bible a record of man's encounter with God, but it also contains God's revelation of truth to man. God acts in history and then gives us an infallible interpretation of those acts. For these theologians, however, regardless of what the hidden humanistic assumptions are, the end product is that the Bible is ignored or attacked.

In opposition to this, we state without hesitation that the Bible is the final authority in all matters of doctrine and morals. We are to speak where the Bible speaks and to be silent when the Bible is silent. Speculation is not the way to do theology. The historical and grammatical exegesis of relevant passages in Scripture is the only safe path for those who look to God as the Origin of truth.

Humanistic thinkers have a totally different approach to truth. They assume that:

1. Man is the origin of truth and morals, not God.

2. Man can be the final judge of truth and morals when some part of his being is absolutized, made into the origin of meaning, and everything else is reduced to it.

3. Man's reason, feelings, or experiences are absolutized and are made into rationalism, mysticism, and empiricism.

4. Our conception of God is accordingly to be derived from what man thinks, feels, or experiences.

5. The Bible is not the *final* authority. The Bible is to be accepted to the degree it agrees with our reason, feelings, or experiences.

This approach to truth and morals is particularly dangerous because it forms the basis of the truth claims of the New Age Movement. New Age leaders such as Shirley MacLaine do not hesitate to claim that their ideas about religion are true because they have *experienced* them. On this basis we are told that reincarnation is true, that man is a god, etc.

The Christian who bases his doctrines on his reason, feelings, or experience has no way to counter someone whose reason, feelings, or experience tells him that witchcraft is good. Once we assume that "man is the measure of all things," then all our beliefs become relative and subjective. Religion is reduced to "paying your nickel and taking your choice." Religious truth as *truth* becomes a farce.

In this light, it has become necessary to remind evangelicals that there is a distinctively Christian way of knowing truth that does not fall into rationalism, mysticism, or empiricism. It is historically known as Biblicism. It assumes that:

1. God is the Origin of truth and morals, not man.

2. God's revelation in Scripture is the final authority in all matters of doctrine and morals.

3. Man's reason, feelings, and experiences are not to be viewed as the origin or final judge of truth, justice, morals, or beauty.

4. The Bible contains propositional truths that give us facts about God, the world He made, man's origin, Fall, and need of salvation. Revelation contains inerrant information as well as providing a record of man's experience with God.

5. The only *valid* way to find out such things as whether God knows the future is to examine what the Scriptures have to say on the issue. What someone's reason, intuition, feelings, or experiences have to say on the subject has no ultimate bearing on the issue whatsoever.

6. It really does not matter to us if someone feels comfortable or uncomfortable with what the Bible teaches. The basis of historic Christianity, Reformation theology, and evangelical doctrine is the whole Bible and nothing but the Bible, so help us God.

With these few introductory words, let us examine the truth claims of rationalism, mysticism, and empiricism in the light of the infallible and inerrant Word of God.

Rationalism

One of the greatest challenges the Church faces today is the rationalism which grew out of the humanism of the Renaissance during the fifteenth and sixteenth centuries in Western Europe. The philosopher Descartes is usually designated as the "Father" of modern rationalism because he believed that while he could doubt the existence of God, the world, other people, and even his own body, there was one thing that he could not doubt: that *he* existed — because he was the one doubting!

Descartes thus began with *himself* and tried to work up to an explanation of the existence and form of the universe and the nature of God. He assumed that man could start from himself, by himself, without any outside revelation from God, and still come to a true understanding of the world around him. He began with man and not God because he assumed that "man is the measure of all things" including God, truth, and morals.

Descartes was following the same path that unbelief has always taken. Some aspect of man was abstracted from his being and made into the origin of truth. Man's feelings, experience, or reason took the place that God alone can occupy. In this case, the rationalists took human reason and turned it into an ideal, abstract, absolute, transcendent "Reason" which was the origin, basis, and judge of all truth.

To the rationalist, "reality" is limited to what *he* thinks it to be in *his* own mind. Whatever is "unthinkable" to *him* cannot be true or even exist. He assumes that he can simply sit down in a dark room and through "Reason" alone come to understand everything. Divine revelation is not needed.

The rationalists developed various phrases and slogans that expressed the supremacy of reason. All ideas must be "in accord with reason." They must be "tried before the bar of reason." Any idea that does not "satisfy the demands of reason" must be rejected. All ideas must "justify themselves before reason." Philosophy begins and ends with the "first principles of reason." They also appeal to such words as "intuition," "intelligent," "logical," and "educated," as if anyone who disagrees with them is obviously stupid.

Rationalists do not hesitate to demand that such things as the existence of God and the inspiration of the Bible must be "justified before the bar of reason." They will accept the Bible only insofar as it is "in agreement with reason."

The Mysteries of the Faith

Rationalists have always attacked certain Christian doctrines as being "irrational" and "incoherent" because they are "mysteries" of the faith. They gleefully denounce such doctrines as the Trinity, the foreknowledge of God, the sovereignty of God, the imputation of Adam's sin, election and predestination, creation, the inerrancy of Scripture, and Christ's substitutionary atonement as "not in accord with reason."

They demand to know "how" God can be one and three at the same time, foreknow the future, and be the sovereign Creator and Sustainer of all things? How can the imputation of Adam's sin to us, our sin to Christ on the cross, and His righteousness to us be "justified before reason." Since they don't see how God's sovereignty and human responsibility can both be true, they simply throw out God's sovereignty. Everything must be reduced to their idea of what is "reasonable."

If they can't understand something, it is rejected. If they must choose between the "free will" of man and the "free will" of God, they always exalt man and dethrone God. Man becomes the measure of all things, including religious ideas. This is the heart and soul of religious humanism.

Is Reason Really Sufficient?

The problem with appealing to "reason" as the sole basis of truth is that it is not infallible and hence it is not as trustworthy as rationalists assume. Also, each rationalist has his own personal tastes and prejudices in view when he speaks of "reason" with hushed tones. Rationalists have always disagreed among themselves as to whose "reason" is ultimate. Each one in turn tries to claim the honor for himself and to refute all the rationalists who went before him. No wonder rationalism fell into disgrace in secular philosophy!

We wish that we could say that rationalism perished from off the face of the earth many years ago. But, sad to say, we have encountered more committed rationalists in the Christian Church than we have found in the world. Religious rationalists are always difficult to nail down because no matter how many Biblical passages you show them in support of a doctrine, they can always wave them aside in the name of "reason." Because they don't see how this or that doctrine can be reconciled in their mind with another doctrine, they will pick one and reject the other. But in all their picking, *man* always comes out on top.

The Role of Human Reason in Scripture

The first thing that strikes the reader of the Bible is the conspicuous absence of any reference to any abstract concept of "Reason." The authors of Scripture never claimed that their doctrines were true because they were "reasonable." They never referred to or viewed human reason as "the ultimate court of appeal." They never demanded belief or obedience "in the name of reason." And, at no time did they ever justify their teachings "before the bar of reason."

The various Hebrew and Greek words that are translated as "reason" in our English versions always refer either to sanity or to common sense (Daniel 4:36; Acts 6:2 *KJV*). Since the abstract concept of "Reason" was not developed until the Renaissance, this is to be expected.

Instead of seeking to justify Divine revelation before human reason, the authors of Scripture always demanded that human reason justify itself before revelation! Human reason was correct to the degree it agreed with revelation and not the other way around.

Moses is a good example of the way Biblical writers viewed human reason. He began the Bible with the existence of God (Genesis 1:1). He did not begin with an attempt to justify the existence of God before man's reason. Moses did the exact opposite. He justified the existence of man on the basis of the existence of God! When Moses gave the Law to Israel he never said, "Do this because it is reasonable." He said, "Do this because God said so." The supremacy was always given to revealed truth.

That the authors of Scripture viewed Divine revelation as the ultimate court of appeal is clearly seen from the way they handled all conflicts between human reason and revelation. Whenever a conflict arose between human reason and revelation, human reason was rebuked as rebellious (see Romans 9:10-21).

Indeed, even if all of mankind were to rise up and call a certain revealed truth "irrational," "not in accord with reason," "unjust," or even "wicked," the Apostle Paul said, "Let God be true and every man a liar" (Romans 3:4). It is interesting to note in passing that when Paul in the book of Romans had to deal with the conflict between sinful human reason and revealed truth, the focus of controversy was usually the doctrine of God's sovereignty (see Romans 3:1-19; 9:1-33; 11:1-36). The rejection of this Biblical doctrine is viewed as rebellion against God.

Throughout Scripture, man is viewed as the *receiver* of truth and morals and not its creator. God is the Author of all truth and morals and the Source of all wisdom and knowledge (see 2 Chronicles 1:10-12; Proverbs 1:1-7; Daniel 1:17; 2:23; John 1:17; Romans 1:25; James 1:5).

The Limitations of Reason

"Reason" cannot be viewed as the origin or judge of truth because of inescapable Biblical realities. First, human reason is finite. Thus it is not an infinite reference point, which can give meaning to the particulars of life. Second, human reason is sinful. It cannot be trusted, according to the Bible. Third, man's mind is not capable of an exhaustive understanding of truth or morals. We can only go so far before our reason "runs out of steam."

The intrinsic limitations of human reason forever disqualify it as the origin or final judge of truth. It is thus not surprising in the least to find that revealed truth goes beyond the ability of the human mind to understand. Indeed, if the human mind could understand everything the Bible teaches, this would prove that the Scriptures were of human origin and not inspired by God!

The fact that the Bible goes *beyond* human reason does not mean that it goes *against* rationality or logic. The seeming contradictions and irreconcilable truths found in Scripture only point us to the Infinite Mind who gave it. Man's failure to understand completely the truths revealed in Scripture does not imply an inherent irrationality in God or His revelation. It simply shows the limitation of our minds."

In reality, there are no inherent contradictions in God or His Word. Some of the truths of the Bible are incapable of human reconciliation because we don't have all the facts before us and our minds are not capable of understanding anything in an exhaustive way. But faith can always swim when reason can no longer feel the bottom.

The person committed to the supremacy and sufficiency of Scripture is not bothered by the fact that he cannot completely understand or explain the doctrine of the Trinity, the decrees of God, creation, original sin, predestination, or the atonement. They are called "mysteries" in Scripture because they are truths that did not originate in the mind of man and that he cannot fully understand. In the Old Testament, the passage that fully sets out the finite nature of human reason is found in Job 38-40. (See also Job 5:9; 11:7-9). In the New Testament, the same doctrine is taught in Romans 11:33-36; Ephesians 3:8, 19 and Philippians 4:7.

Revelation Goes Beyond Reason

The Christian is not under any Biblical constraint whatsoever to justify revealed truth before the bar of a mythological "reason" created by rationalists. For example, the doctrine of the Trinity is *true* because it is a *revealed* truth. It is not true because it is "reasonable." It is reasonable because it is true!

As a revealed truth, the doctrine of the Trinity is not irrational, unreasonable, or antilogical. The failure of our reason and logic to explain everything about the Trinity reveals our finiteness. Being infinite, God does not have any such difficulties and He understands His Triune nature completely.

Human reason is not only finite but also corrupted and twisted by sin. Thus the human mind or heart is morally incapable of submitting to revealed truth. Christian theologians speak of the "noetic effects of the Fall," by which they mean the effects of sin on the human mind and thinking ability. The noetic effects of the Fall focus on a moral problem of man. To put it bluntly, by nature man is *biased* against God and His Law/Word (Romans 8:7). Man's depravity is moral and not physical or metaphysical.

As soon as Adam and Eve fell into sin, their reason became darkened and they thought and did the most wicked and stupid things" (Genesis 3:8-12). How then can man be the final judge of truth when he is biased against God to begin with? By nature we are "children of wrath" who "hate the light and love darkness" (John 3:19-20, Ephesians 2:1-3).

All the same, the moral implications of the Fall should not be twisted to mean that man's ability to think logically or rationally was destroyed by Adam's Fall into sin. Man is still in the image of God (James 3:9) and can still know that $1 + 1 = 2$ or that the law of noncontradiction is true. Man's rationality, like fire, must be kept in its place. But when man's rationality is made the alpha and the omega of all knowledge, it becomes destructive. Thus we have no problems *per se* with human reason as a finite reflection of the rational mind of God. But when reason is exalted into "Reason," it becomes a false god and serves as an example of man's propensity to idolatry.

The Mind and Heart of Man

In Scripture, the mind, heart, and conscience of man is described in the following ways:

- evil (Genesis 6:5; 8:21)
- corrupt and vile (Psalm 14:1-3)
- futile (Psalm 94:11)
- senseless (Jeremiah 10:14)
- deceptive above all things (Jeremiah 17:9)
- beyond cure (Jeremiah 17:9)
- hostile to the Light (John 3:19-20)
- suppressing the truth (Romans 1:18)
- darkened (Romans 1:21)
- foolish (Romans 1:22)
- idolatrous (Romans 1:23-26)
- carnal (Romans 8:6)
- dead (Romans 8:6)
- rebellious and hostile to God and His Law (Romans 8:7)
- incapable of pleasing God (Romans 8:8)
- blinded by Satan (2 Corinthians 4:3-4)
- corrupted (2 Corinthians 11:3; 1 Timothy 6:5; 2 Timothy 3:8)
- futile and darkened (Ephesians 4:17-19)
- unspiritual (Colossians 2:18)

- defiled (Titus 1:15)

The New Testament describes the total depravity of human reason in Romans 1:18-32. In this passage, Paul says that the mind of man suppresses the truth revealed by God in both general and special revelation. He says that man's reason is without excuse, futile, foolish, darkened, idolatrous, sinful, immoral, depraved, and full of hate toward God. He describes what man is really like if God does not intervene by His sovereign grace.

Summary

Since human reason is finite and has been corrupted by sin, we must not "lean on our own understanding" or "be wise in our own eyes" (Proverbs 3:5-7). Human reason must bow before Scripture and admit that some things revealed in it "transcend all understanding" (see Philippians 4:7).

God's revelation is "unsearchable" and it "surpasses all understanding" (Ephesians 3:8, 19). We must confess with the Psalmist that such knowledge is "too wonderful" and "too lofty" and "cannot be fathomed" by the mind of man (Psalm 139:6; 145:3).

> For who has understood the mind of the Lord, or instructed Him as His counselor (Isaiah 40:13; 1 Corinthians 2:16)?

The Role of Human Reason in Theology

Having seen that human reason is not the abstract and absolute "Reason" found in the myths of the rationalists, we must emphasize that one can be rational without being a rationalist. We can use reason without absolutizing it into the origin and judge of all truth. Human reason is to function as the *servant* of revelation and not its judge. Once man's reason bows to the supremacy of God's Reason, then it is set free to be what God intended it to be.

In God's wondrous work of salvation, He illuminates, regenerates, and renews the corrupt mind of man which has been darkened by sin and blinded by Satan (2 Corinthians 4:4-6; Matthew 16:17; Ephesians 1:18; John 3:3, 5; Romans 12:2). Once the mind is set free from its bondage to sin and guilt, it is then ready to fulfill its role by studying God's revelation in nature and in Scripture. We are to use our minds to plumb its depths and scale its heights; to clarify and refine its concepts; to discover its principles; to obey its commands; and to defend its truthfulness. This is God's plan for man's reason according to Genesis 2:19-20.

Logic and the Bible

We can use logic as a tool without being a rationalist because logic itself finds its ontological basis in the nature of the Creator of all things. In terms of its nature, a particular principle of human logic is valid if it reflects the Mind of God as revealed in Scripture. Logic thus has an ontological basis and is not to be reduced to a relative and cultural psychology.

Man was made in the image of God, and part of this image is his capacity for logical thought, which is simply thinking God's thoughts after Him. While man's understanding is finite, it is nevertheless *true* because it comes from the image of God within him. Thus 1 + 1 = 2 is true for both God and man with the main difference being that God understands it infinitely and man finitely.

A close study of Scripture reveals that logic is used to convey, clarify, and defend revealed truth because it finds its own validity in God's nature. For example, the "law of non-contradiction" is rooted in the very Being of the God who cannot lie (Titus 1:2). When Paul said that God cannot both be God and a lying God at the same time, he was actually saying:

$$\sim [\, a \wedge \bar{a}\,]$$

The rule of logic which is called "the denial of the consequence" is used in such places as Galatians 5:18-21; 1 Corinthians 6:9-11; 2 Corinthians 5:17, etc. In such places, Paul did not hesitate to argue:

> If someone is in union with Christ, then he will be a new creature.
> *If someone is not a new creature*, then he is not in union with Christ.

The Apostle Paul had no problem whatsoever "reasoning" from the Scriptures (Acts 17:2; 18:4, 19, etc.). In all his writings, Paul constantly used logically valid forms of argumentation to demonstrate from the Old Testament that Jesus was the Messiah.

We must also remember that although human logic can tell us if the structure of an argument is *valid*, it cannot tell us if it is *true*. Indeed, an argument can be logically valid and materially false at the same time! Observe the following example.

- *Premise 1:* Something which is correct part of the time is better than something which is never correct.

- *Premise 2:* A stopped watch is correct twice a day while a fast or slow watch is *never correct.*

- *Conclusion:* It is better to wear a stopped watch than one that is fast or slow.

The above argument is logically valid but false! While something that is true will always be logically valid, the converse is not the case.

The logic or Logos of God is Jesus Christ, the Second Person of the Trinity. As the personification of divine logic, Jesus is the servant of the Lord and He does not sit in judgment on Divine Truth but seeks to serve it with reverence and humility. This is the true role of human reason.

Mysticism

One of the most perplexing problems we face today is the resurgence of mysticism in the Church of the twentieth century. We are encountering more people everyday who choose their views of God and His salvation solely on the basis of their "feelings." They do theology on the basis of, "If an idea *feels* good, we believe it."

The History of Mysticism

As a distinct philosophy, mysticism arose out of the humanism of the Renaissance. In mysticism, the emotions or the feelings of man are isolated from the rest of his being and then absolutized into the origin of all meaning and the basis and judge of all truth. Thus the "feelings" of man become the measure of all things, including truth, justice, morals, and beauty. Whatever feels "good" or "comfortable" is assumed to be true.

Most mystics have come to the depressing conclusion that a rational understanding of the universe is not really possible. Neither can the universe be understood by experimentation as the empiricists claim. There must be some other way of knowing the truth than by human reason or experience.

One would have hoped that having seen the futility of beginning with man's reason or experience as the measure of all things, they would have realized that the root problem was *beginning* with man in the first place.

The book of Ecclesiastes teaches us that when we begin with finite man, we always end in skepticism (i.e., we cannot know truth from error) and relativism (i.e., we cannot know good from evil). Everything becomes vanity or emptiness.

The humanists have always begun with man as a self-sufficient being who does not need God's grace or revelation. Instead of looking away from themselves to the God who made them, they turned to what they thought was a "new way" of knowing. This new way was to look within themselves for the truth.

Although this notion had served as the basis of Eastern religions for thousands of years, the idea that truth could be found by simply "looking within" themselves to their emotions was quite new to the men of the Renaissance. This meant that they did not need a great intellect or vast scientific experience to understand the universe. Man's heart, i.e., his feelings, was the best guide to what was good, just, and true.

To the Christian, the idea that we should trust our heart to tell us the truth is foolish, for God has warned us, "the heart is deceitful above all things and desperately wicked" (Jeremiah 17:9).

The question as to how one went about "looking within" himself proved to be a tricky problem. Some said that truth could be found only after various ceremonies such as fasting or prayer. Others said that they instantly knew the truth when they heard it because their hearts felt a certain chill when the truth was being expressed. Still others required people to go into trances before the truth could be found.

The mystics could never agree as to how to "look within" yourself, and neither could they agree as to what is good, just, or true. These problems proved to be insurmountable. Mysticism fell into disrepute as the mystics fought among themselves over whose feelings were the ultimate judge of truth.

While mysticism is no longer a popular philosophy in the world, it is alive and well in the Christian Church. Indeed, it has become a dominant force in some Christian circles. Christian mystics identify themselves by their dependence on feelings for their doctrines and morals. And this is where the problem lies.

Mystics and the Bible

The Bible clearly teaches that our doctrines and morals should arise from a careful study of the Scriptures (2 Timothy 2:15; 3:16-17). But instead of studying the Bible to see what it says, the mystic will try to "feel" his way to the Truth. He is not interested in a careful study of the text of Scripture. He is only interested in how he "feels." He assumes that truth will conform itself to what his feelings tell him is true or false, right or wrong.

When confronted with a doctrine he does not like, such as original sin, a mystic will usually say something like:

> My feelings tell me that this doctrine is not true. I feel uncomfortable with the very idea. So, I must reject it.

The mystic is not saying that he will examine Scripture and let Scripture decide his doctrines. In reality, his doctrines come from his mysterious "feelings" which, supposedly tell him truth from error and right from wrong.

Whenever you hear someone saying that he will "pray about it" in order for him to "feel" what the Lord "says" to him "in his heart," you are dealing with a mystic. This person is assuming that truth is discovered by looking to his feelings instead of reading the Scriptures!

As a way of obtaining doctrine, morals, or guidance, mysticism has a poor track record. If the truth can be known through feelings, then all mystics should perceive the same truth. But there is nothing more fickle than human emotion. Thus the mystics always disagree among themselves, and the same mystic will change his mind as many times as his feelings change.

Human Emotion in Scripture and Theology

In Scripture, neither reason nor emotion is the determining factor in doctrine or morals. Not once did God ask people how they *felt* about His Laws. They were to obey regardless of their feelings. Revealed truth was never said to be true because someone felt good or comfortable about it. As a matter of fact, the history of the people of God as given in Scripture reveals that people did not generally *like* God's laws at all. And they certainly had some very bad feelings about the judgment of God on their sins.

Human emotion cannot be the measure of all things because it is finite. It is therefore insufficient as a basis for truth. It is not only finite but also sinful, according to Scripture (Genesis 6:5; Romans 3:10-18). Our emotions are hostile to God and our hearts actually hate God (Romans 1:30; 8:7). Our hearts are deceitful and cannot be trusted (Jeremiah 17:9). We do not want the light of truth but the darkness of error because our deeds are evil (John 3:19-21). No one seeks after or understands the true God (Romans 3:11).

Whenever a conflict arose between human emotion and revealed truth, the authors of Scripture rebuked that emotion as rebellion against God (Romans 9:14-23). It also comes as no surprise to find that it was over such humbling doctrines as God's sovereignty that sinful emotions rose up against God (Romans 4:4-8; 9:14-23; Psalm 2:1-12).

Just because we do not "like" a doctrine or we are not "comfortable" with it does not mean that it is not true. Most of the doctrines of Scripture are very hard on the emotions of man. We are told that we are wicked sinners on our way to an eternal hell which we justly deserve. Our pride is trampled to the dust and the Holy Spirit makes us feel guilty and afraid. Nevertheless, the doctrines of the sinfulness of man and the justice of hell are clearly taught in the Bible.

Does this mean that there is no place for human emotion in the Christian life? Of course not! We can state that human emotion has a role to play without becoming a mystic. It is the attempt to make emotions into an idol to which we object.

Human emotions such as guilt and fear are often the very means God uses to bring us to true repentance (2 Corinthians 7:10). The joy of His salvation comes to us at conversion (Psalm 51:12). Emotion has a very powerful role to play in the salvation of lost sinners. Until they feel as well as understand their need of salvation, they will not seek the Lord.

Emotion plays a powerful role in the Christian life. In the Psalms, we find human emotion in all its forms from the heights of joy to the depths of depression (Psalm 6; cf. Psalm 8). There are "songs in the night" as well as "joy in the morning." There is an appropriate Psalm for every occasion and condition of the human heart. This is why it is the favorite prayer book and hymn book of true Christians.

Throughout the Scriptures, "happiness depends on happenings," i.e., our emotional state usually depends on the circumstances around us. In some times and situations, we should sorrow and weep (Romans 12:15; 1 Corinthians 12:26; James 4:9-10). Even Jesus wept at the grave of Lazarus (John 11:35). The idea that Christians have to be happy all the time violates Scripture as well as sound human psychology. It burdens the people of God with an impossible task. It leads to a kind of hypocrisy that drives the unsaved away from the Gospel. We must not wear a mask of happiness when we are sick, sinful, or sorrowful.

While "happiness" comes and goes with the ebb and flow of daily events and can be affected by such things as the level of sugar, iron, or calcium in the blood, monthly cycles, personal tragedy, amount of sleep, etc., our ability to "thank God for everything" remains firm because giving thanks is an act of the will and not an emotion. Regardless of how we feel, we are to trust God and thank Him that He knows "why" things happen. We can commit our souls to our Maker and trust His sovereign will (1 Thessalonians 5:18).

Certain emotions such as joy, peace, patience, etc., should be cultivated in the Christian life (Galatians 5:22-23). Sinful emotions such as lust, anger, envy, hate, etc., should be "put to death" or "put off" (Romans 8:13; Colossians 3:8-9).

We should express our emotions in public and private worship (Psalm 150). The idea that "emotions" are intrinsically bad and should never be expressed in the worship of God flows out of the Greek deification of the mind and not from the Scriptures. Human emotions are never condemned in Scripture because they are *human* or because they are *emotions*. Only if an emotion was *sinful* (hate, lust, etc.) was it condemned.

The Lord Jesus expressed every valid emotion of the human heart without sin being involved at any point. We should never be ashamed of our tears or our laughter because the Lord Jesus Christ Himself wept and rejoiced openly.[1]

Summary

Human emotion must be made the servant of the Lord. As a humble servant, it will not try to judge truth or be the origin of morals. Instead of looking within ourselves, we need to look away from ourselves to God, His Word, and His grace. Instead of conforming Scripture to our feelings, we need to conform our feelings to Scripture. We need to trust in the Lord and His Word instead of trusting in our deceitful feelings.

Empiricism

Humanism has always taught that man is the measure of all things. Thus man's experience has been viewed by some as the origin of all truth. We can know what is true, just, and moral from human experience. Thus there is no need for Divine revelation. Man can discover the truth by himself.

This humanist view gave rise to such principles as:

- If it works, it's true.
- The end justifies the means.

That such principles should be utilized by unbelievers is not surprising. But when we find Christians using such principles as the basis of their doctrines and morals, it is scandalous.

Humanism has always rested on the doctrine of human autonomy, i.e., man has everything he needs within himself. He does not need God, or His Word, or His Grace. Man is self-sufficient. Man is his own god.

Humanism can express itself in religious terms as easily as in secular terminology. There are those within the Church of the twentieth century who boldly teach that man is his own "god." Man has all the power he needs within himself. The "free will" of man is absolute and thus he is not a helpless sinner in need of God's intervention by way of revelation or grace.

The only way that these Christian humanists can exalt man is by dethroning God. Instead of man's being dependent on God, God is said to be dependent on man! It is said that God is helpless and impotent. He is not allowed to intervene or to interfere with the affairs of almighty man. This "God" is a poor, pathetic being who deserves our pity. Man is on the throne now and God waits to do his bidding. God has been reduced to being a mere puppet with man pulling the strings.

One of the clearest expressions of humanistic pragmatism is found in the idea that truth and morals depend on one's personal experiences. Instead of studying Scripture to see what God has revealed, the Christian humanist will base his beliefs on human experience.

An Example of Religious Empiricism

One example comes to mind which clearly illustrates this problem. The following is a dialogue between Sam and Bob over the issue of being "slain in the Spirit."

> Sam: Oh, what a wonderful time I had last night in church! I was "slain in the Spirit" and I must have lain there at least an hour. When Kathryn touched me, I felt the electricity of the Spirit and it knocked me down flat. Isn't that wonderful?

> Bob: I'm glad that you had a wonderful time in church but I'm not altogether sure that this "slain in the Spirit" stuff is Scriptural.

> Sam: Don't be silly! Of course it is true, because I *experienced* it and a lot of other people have experienced it too. And, it felt

so good to be slain. Kathryn came by me and I reached out and touched the hem of her garment and down I went. What could possibly be wrong with that?

Bob: But where in the Bible or church history do you find this stuff? Aren't you concerned in the least if "being slain" is true according to God's Word? We must not interpret the Bible according to our experience. Instead, we must interpret our experience according to the Bible. Wouldn't you agree?

Sam: I don't see what you are getting all hyper about. I know it is true because I experienced it. I don't have to run around and prove it by the Bible or church history. But I'll ask my pastor for the proof tonight and I'll tell you tomorrow.

The next day . . .

Bob: Well, what did your pastor say?

Sam: He told me that I should not talk to you anymore. He said that you are guilty of something called "bibliolatry" because you think that the Bible is God.

Bob: But I don't think that the Bible is God and neither do I worship it as God. But the Bible does tell us that what we believe and how we live are to come from it and not from human experience. I guess that he could not come up with any proof and just told you to avoid me.

Sam: No, he gave me all the proof I needed. Being "slain in the Spirit" is clearly taught in John 18:6 and Revelation 1:17. There! Does that satisfy you?

Bob: I don't really think that you can legitimately use those passages. First, let me ask you something. Was being "slain in the Spirit" a blessing or a judgment of God?

Sam: It's a wonderful blessing! I know because I experienced it.

Bob: But if this is so, how can you use John 18:6, when in that passage Jesus judged his enemies who were coming to kill him by knocking them down? Furthermore, they did not become unconscious. It was also a very unpleasant experience for them. Remember, this was not a worship service! Jesus did not touch them. As a matter of fact, in the Gospels whenever Jesus touched people, or they touched him, no one ever got knocked down.

Sam: Well, I must admit that John 18 doesn't exactly prove my case but Revelation 1:17 does.

Bob: Sam, did you bother to look at the text at all? It isn't enough to cite a verse. You have to examine it. Was there a worship service going on? Did an evangelist touch him? If you read the text you will find that John actually fainted in fright. He was so frightened by the appearance of Jesus that he fainted. Are you going to say that whenever someone faints in fright that this is what "slain in the Spirit" is all about? I thought you told me it was a pleasant experience. Did you faint in fright the other night?

Sam: You are doing exactly what my pastor said you would do. He warned me that you would try to rob me of my experience.

Bob: But Sam, all I did was to look at the context and the wording of those passages. Isn't this what we are supposed to do as Christians?

Sam: I'm not going to talk about it anymore with you. I know I am right because I experienced it and you could show me all the verses in the Bible until you are blue in the face and I still will not believe you.

This illustration is based upon an actual conversation. Although we do not deny that Sam was "saved," in his thinking he was still a humanist because he assumed that his experience was the measure of truth. He did not need the Bible to tell him right from wrong, or truth from error. It did not matter what the issue was. It could be tongues, worship, healing, salvation, or God's foreknowledge. In all these issues his experience was ultimate.

Human Experience in Scripture and Theology

Human experience is never appealed to in Scripture as the basis or judge of truth or morals. Since our experiences need to be interpreted and understood, how can they serve as the basis for anything? The real issue is, "How do we interpret our experiences?"

The humanist will interpret his experiences according to what he thinks or feels that they mean to him. He does not go outside of himself for an interpretation. For example, Saul went to the Witch of Endor because others had gone there and experienced what they claimed was communication with the dead (1 Samuel 28). So, he went and asked her to call up Samuel. After the seance, Saul thought that he had talked with Samuel.

Now, the theist will not trust his reason or emotions to interpret his experiences (Proverbs 3:5-7). Instead, he goes outside of himself to God's Word to seek an explanation. In the case of Saul, we would interpret Saul's experience at Endor differently from the way he did. On the basis of other texts of Scripture, such as Deuteronomy 18:9-14, we would say that Saul was actually talking to a demon who pretended to be Samuel. Saul was deceived and tricked by the old witch.

Now, no one denies that Saul had an experience. The issue comes down to how we interpret it. The humanist will look to himself for the interpretation, while the theist will look to Scripture (2 Timothy 3:16-17).

Truth and morals cannot be decided by our experience, because each experience itself must be judged as to whether it is true, just, or moral according to Scripture. Just because something works, gets the job done, or feels good, does not mean that it is true, just, or moral (Deuteronomy 13:1-5). The ends do not justify the means (Romans 6:1-2). We must interpret our experiences according to the Word of God.

> To the Law and to the Testimony! If they do not speak according to this Word, they have no light (Isaiah 8:20).

Divine Revelation

God has chosen in His sovereign mercy to reveal Himself to a fallen humanity. He was under no obligation to do so, because we all have sinned against His grace and provoked Him to His face (Romans 3:23). We have trampled His Law under our feet. The only thing God owes us is eternal punishment!

How did God reveal Himself? In Paul's Epistle to the Romans, he points out that all men are without excuse and are under the wrath of Almighty God because they have rejected God's revelation. This revelation is twofold: general and special.

General Revelation

There is, first of all, the general revelation of God as found in the creation around us and our conscience within us. The existence and form of the universe are such that, what

> is known about God is evident within them; for God made it evident to them. For since the creation of the world His invisible attributes, His eternal power and divine nature, have been clearly seen, being understood through what has been made, so that they are without excuse (Romans 1:19-20).

Again,

> The heavens are telling of the glory of God; and the firmament is declaring the work of His hands (Psalm 19:1).

General revelation from the creation around us is going on twenty-four hours a day, seven days a week, in every part of creation; to every human being. It does not matter if man through his own wickedness has blinded himself to the light of creation, the light is still shining.

> Day to day pours forth speech; and night to night reveals knowledge (Psalm 19:2).

Not only does the existence and form of the universe reveal the hand of the Creator, but the uniqueness of man as particularly displayed in his conscience reveals that the Creator is also the Law-Giver and Judge.

> For when Gentiles who do not have the Law do instinctively the things of the Law, these, not having the Law, are a law to themselves, in that they show the work of the Law written in their hearts, their conscience bearing witness, and their thoughts alternately accusing or else defending themselves (Romans 2:14-15).

The conscience of man, although defiled and scarred by sin, reveals that man is not a brute beast kicked up by some unlucky fluke of a meaningless and purposeless evolutionary process. He is the image-bearer of God.

Special Revelation

Psalm 19 moves from general revelation (vv. 1-6) to special revelation (vv. 7-11) as David considers the revelatory nature of the Holy Scriptures. In the same way, having spoken of creation in Romans 1 and conscience in Romans 2, the Apostle Paul in Romans 3 speaks of the "oracles of God" as given in Scripture.

General revelation cannot save anyone, for it does not reveal salvation or the Savior. Paul argues that creation and conscience can only bring us into further condemnation. By these things we know that we are creatures of God who are in rebellion against Him and under His wrath. That is all.

It is only in special revelation that we are told of a way to escape the just judgment of the Creator on rebel sinners. The Scriptures reveal the truth about God, man, and salvation. They tell us in language that cannot be misunderstood that we are in need of salvation and a Savior. Man cannot "go it alone."

The Bible is God's infallible and inerrant written Word just as much as Jesus was the infallible and inerrant Living Word. The two Words are one in that Jesus is the Speaker and His words, the Scriptures. As the divine Logos (John 1:1), Jesus is the basis of all revelation, particularly propositional revelation. He forms the point of contact or bridge between the infinite mind of God and the finite mind of man. Jesus can do this because He is *both* God and man.

The full authority of Scripture rests on the fact that it is "God breathed" (2 Timothy 3:16). Because it comes from an infallible and inerrant God, it is,

> profitable for teaching, for reproof, for correction, for training in righteousness; that the man of God may be adequate, equipped for every good work (2 Timothy 3:16-17).

Conclusion

Why depend on the quagmire of "reason" when we have a sure foundation in Scripture? Why follow the fantasies of "feelings" when we have the facts of Scripture? And why be deceived by "experience" when the truth has been revealed in Scripture?

The Bible never changes. It is not caught up in any "process." Its truths are immutable and infallible. Its words are "perfect" (Psalm 19:7) and come from the Holy Spirit as He moved the prophets of old (1 Corinthians 2:13; 2 Peter 1:21).

What is God like? Is He infinite in His nature and attributes? Has God revealed Himself or are we left to the conceit of our own vain speculations? Does God know the future? Is He the Creator of space and time or do they create Him?

Thanks be unto God for He has made Himself known in Scripture! His Word is the final judge of truth, justice, morals, and beauty. Its doctrines shall stand long after the cavillings of rationalists, mystics, and empiricists, secular or religious, have long been forgotten.

To God be all the glory!

Questions for Discussion

1. From where are to derive our knowledge of God? Are to look "within ourselves" to see what our reason or feelings tell us? Or, are we to look outside of ourselves to the Bible as the source of an accurate knowledge of God?

2. Where do liberal theologians, the cults and the occult get their ideas of God?

3. What is "rationalism" and does it work? Have you ever met a rationalist? What kinds of things did he say about God?

4. What is "mysticism" and does it work? Have you ever met people who try to find the truth by feelings? What did they say about God?

5. What is "empiricism" and does it work? Have you ever met someone who argued that sometime is true because they experienced it?

TWO

THE DANGER
OF IDOLATRY

In Christian theology, God is a theological "Given" who has revealed Himself in Scripture. Thus we are *not* free to "pick and choose" among the attributes of God as if we were in an ice cream parlor. What God is like in His nature and attributes is *not* left to our personal tastes.

Humanistic thinkers assume that they are "free" to reject any attribute of God that they cannot fully understand, completely explain, rationally reconcile, and feel happy about. If they don't *like* a certain attribute of God, they have no qualms about throwing it out. But God demands that we accept Him as He has revealed Himself in Scripture. Anything less than this is a rejection of God.

The God who has chosen to reveal Himself in Scripture is a very jealous God. He condemns as idolatry any attempt to add to or subtract from His revealed nature. This is so important that God devoted the first two Commandments of the Decalogue to a condemnation of all attempts to mold God into a manmade image. It does not matter if the image is mental or metal, wooden or woolly, all manmade ideas of God are idolatry.

The First Commandment

In the First Commandment God tells us, "You shall have no other gods before Me" (Exodus 20:3).

In this commandment we find that:

1. There is only one God.

2. The God who has revealed Himself in Scripture is this God.

3. He alone is to be worshiped, feared, loved, and obeyed.

4. We are not free to make up any ideas on our own of what God is like. It does not matter if our ideas seem "reasonable" or "practical" to us. We cannot have any ideas of God except those revealed in Scripture.

5. Man is not a god-maker or a god-in-the-making. Any concept of the "divinity of man" is idolatrous.

6. God is His own interpreter. He has revealed Himself and interpreted this self-revelation in Scripture.

7. Rationalism, empiricism, mysticism, and all other forms of humanism are hereby condemned as idolatry for they would exalt man's opinion over God's self-revelation as given in Scripture.

The Second Commandment

In the Second Commandment God warns us:

> You shall not make for yourself an idol, or any likeness of what is in heaven above or on the earth beneath or in the water under the earth. You shall not worship them or serve them; for I, the Lord your God, am a jealous God, visiting the iniquity of the fathers on the children, on the third and fourth generations of those who hate Me, but showing lovingkindness to thousands, to those who love Me, and keep My commandments (Exodus 20:4-6).

The text clearly teaches that the greatest evidence of *hatred* toward God is the refusal to accept Him as He has revealed Himself in Scripture. The converse is also true. The greatest evidence of *love* toward God is the acceptance of God as He has revealed Himself in Scripture.

Just as the degree to which we accept revelation is the measure of our love of God, even so the degree to which we follow "reason," "intuition," or "feelings" instead of revelation is the measure of our hatred of God.

Any attempt to construct a deity on the basis of what is palatable to our rational or aesthetic tastes is sheer unmitigated idolatry. Here is no middle ground, no two ways about it, no compromise on this point.

Either we accept God as He has revealed Himself in Scripture or we are idolaters.

This position is quite humbling to fallen man. We don't like the idea of God's *telling* us what He is like. We would much rather make up our own ideas of what God is. Neither do we like the idea of God's *commanding* us to obey Him according to what He says is right or wrong. We would much rather make up our own ideas of what is right and what is wrong.

Haters of God

Our natural hatred of God comes out in our rebellion against His Word and Law. It is no wonder that we find the Apostle Paul describing fallen men as "haters of God" (Romans 1:30). This hatred of God focuses on a rejection of God's revelation in Scripture (Romans 8:7).

The desire to be "free" from God's revelation and God's Law is the very soul and substance of *all* forms of humanism, religious or secular. To a heart filled with hatred toward God, man is not "really" or "genuinely" free unless he can think and do as he pleases as if there were no God or because there is no God. All the humanistic talk about "free will" is nothing more or less than a cheap trick used to deceive Christians.

The Scriptures declare that when man tries to "go it alone" in truth, justice, morals, and beauty, he turns freedom into slavery, liberty into license, good into evil, justice into injustice, truth into error, and beauty into ugliness. All these things can be clearly seen in modern philosophy, theology, and the arts.

But the Christian takes a path to the knowledge of God that is different and more challenging because it takes courage to venture out *beyond* reason and experience into the truths of revelation. Only a bold and daring spirit will be able to cast itself wholly upon God. Only a mighty faith can launch out and swim in unfathomable depths, while those who trust in their reason can only wade in the shallows.

The Loss of Mystery

One of the greatest problems we face in theology today is the lack of any sense of mystery. No one wants to believe in anything that goes beyond the capacity of man to comprehend. Thus the awe and the wonder of the mysteries of God are entirely absent in modern theology. Everything must be explained, sewn up, tied up, and put away in neat little packages.

With the demise of the awe and wonder of mystery in modern theology, faith is not desirable. Humanistic philosophers such as the processians demand "comprehension," not mystery; "coherence," not faith; "reason," not revelation. The absence of true mystery has always been the breeding ground of heresy.

No wonder modern theology is quite arid and sterile. It is insufferably boring. Its world is drab and gray. It is totally bereft of the bright colors of wonder, awe, and mystery. It merely apes the fads of secular philosophy. Thus it is one vast wasteland littered with the bones of those foolish enough to enter it.

But the Bible begins and ends with mystery. Thus the Biblically informed Christian can rejoice in his God. He is not depressed because he can't explain everything and answer every question. He frankly admits that he does not have everything tied up in neat little packages. By faith he can venture out *beyond* the shallows of reason into the uncharted and unfathomable depths of God's mysteries. He is not afraid of accepting by faith alone those mysteries revealed in Scripture.

The word *mystery* is found twenty-seven times in the New Testament. In the Gospels, Jesus often spoke of the "mysteries of the Kingdom" (Matthew 13:11). In the Epistles, Paul uses the word no fewer than twenty times. He spoke of God, His Word, His Will, the Gospel, the Faith, and the Church as "mysteries" (1 Corinthians 4:1; Ephesians 1:9; Colossians 1:26; 1 Timothy 3:9; Ephesians 5:32).

The Biblical concept of "mystery" had no relationship to the Gnostic idea of an esoteric secret told only to an initiated few, as in the ancient mystery religions and modern-day cults and lodges that have secret words, symbols, and rites. The Biblical concept simply meant that God had revealed an idea no human mind ever conceived.

For example, in 1 Corinthians 2:7, Paul speaks of the "mystery" of God's wisdom as displayed in the Gospel. In this passage Paul tells us that this wisdom was a "mystery" because:

1. It was "hidden" from man's sight and perception (v. 7).

2. It was "predestined before the ages to our glory," i.e., it was an idea conceived in the mind of God in eternity before time began (v. 7).

3. It was something "none of the rulers of this age has understood; for if they had understood it, they would not have crucified the

Lord of Glory" (v. 8). If they understood that Christ had come to die according to an eternal predetermined plan, they would have rebelled and refused to murder the Son of God.

4. This mystery was something "which eye has not seen and ear has not heard," i.e., something *beyond* human experience.

5. It contained ideas that "have not entered the heart of man," i.e., things *beyond* human reason and comprehension. This "mystery" was something man could never discover on the basis of his own experience or reason. The only way for man to know of it was through Divine revelation. Thus Paul goes on to say that this was a mystery that "God revealed through the Spirit, not in words taught by human wisdom, but in those taught by the Spirit, combining spiritual thoughts with spiritual words" (vv. 10-13).

Not only is a mystery something man would have never conceived on his own, it is also something that goes beyond his capacity to comprehend. For example, in Ephesians 1:4-11, when Paul touches on God's sovereign will and His decrees of election and predestination, which took place "before the foundation of the world," he speaks of all these things in terms of "the mystery of His will" (v. 9).

Paul speaks of God's electing will as a "mystery." Who can explain how "He is working all things together according to the counsel of His will" and, at the same time, is not the Author of evil? How is it that we are told in James 1:13-14:

> Let no one say when he is tempted, "I am being tempted by God"; for God cannot be tempted by evil, and He Himself does not tempt anyone. But each one is tempted when he is carried away and enticed by his own lust.

Yet, at the same time, we are told to ask God *not* to lead us into temptation (Matthew 6:13)? Or, that God provides us with an escape from the temptation which He also provided (1 Corinthians 10:13)?

Who can fully explain how "God is working *all* things together for our good" (Romans 8:28)? Or how was Judas to blame for betraying the Lord when Jesus said that it "had been determined" by God for him to do it (Luke 22:22)?

What is important for us to understand is that questions relating to God's will and human destiny are placed in the category of "mystery" by the authors of Scripture. Just as the doctrine of the Trinity is a "mystery" and no one will *ever* explain how God can be Three but One and One but Three, neither will anyone cut the "Gordian knot" of Divine sovereignty and man's accountability. Our responsibility is not to pass judgment on revealed truth but to submit to it in awe.

But what if we decide that we will accept only those doctrines of the Bible that "agree with reason"? Those who have an evangelical background will usually reject God's sovereignty, divine election, God's foreknowledge, original sin, and the vicarious nature of the atonement.

But once the principle is laid down that only what is "reasonable" can be accepted, such doctrines as the deity of Christ will have to be rejected, for who can fully explain how Jesus can be *both* God and man? How can one person have *two* natures? Who can make the incarnation "coherent"?

We freely admit that it is a complete mystery to us how Jesus was both God and man. But it is a *revealed* mystery we gladly accept by faith on the authority of Scripture. Why should we abandon the authority of God's Word for the authority of the word of His enemies? But rationalists cannot live in the same universe with mystery.

Conclusion

Over the years we have observed a process of apostasy that begins with the rejection of the mystery of God's sovereignty and then proceeds to the rejecting of the mystery of the inerrancy of Scripture, the authority of Scripture, the incomprehensibility of God, the infinite nature of God, the Trinity, the deity of Christ, the personality and deity of the Holy Spirit, the sinful nature of man, the historicity of Biblical miracles, the accuracy of the Gospel narratives, and the eternal punishment of the wicked.

The driving force that pushes people down this path of apostasy is their refusal to bow in humility before the Word of God. They will not accept the many seemingly conflicting statements of Scripture. They cannot abide mystery in any form. Whatever cannot be rationally explained, they will eventually throw out. They always assume the Greek "either-or" dichotomy in every issue and refuse to acknowledge the "both-and" solution of Scripture because it would throw the issue back into mystery.

We grow weary of hearing that we must choose *either* God's sovereignty *or* man's responsibility. Why is it always assumed that we can't accept *both*? Why do processians assume that if man is free, God must be bound? Why is it assumed that divine election and evangelism cannot both be true? So what if we can't resolve all the questions that humanistic philosophers raise? Ought we not to please God rather than man?

We desire not to judge God's Word but to be judged by it. We strive not to conform the Word to our opinions but our opinions to the Word. We demand not that revelation be in accord with reason but that reason be in accord with revelation. We seek not to master the Bible but to be mastered by it.

Questions for Discussion

1. Can we pick and choose when it comes to the attributes of God.?
2. What if you do not like one of His attributes? Can you throw it out?
3. If everyone's view of God is right, is idolatry possible?
4. Does God care what we think about Him?
5. What does the Bible mean when it talks about "mystery"?

THREE

THE ATTRIBUTES OF GOD

The first thing that must be established is that God has attributes and we can discuss them. This position is clearly based on such Scriptures as Romans 1:20, where the Apostle Paul speaks of God's "attributes."

Secondly, these attributes are not something that man makes up and then projects to God. God has revealed His own attributes in Scripture. Thus we have no choice in the matter whatsoever. We have no freedom to add or subtract to the revealed nature of God. We either accept Him "as is" or reject Him out of hand.

Since God has chosen to reveal Himself in Scripture, the attributes of God found in the Bible are to be accepted by faith and not debated by unbelief. Figure 10.1 on the next page illustrates the nature of the revealed attributes of God.

Humanistic theologies such as processianism assume that God is really unknowable. Since God is unknowable in nature, all His "attributes" are reduced to *man's* subjective and relative descriptions of what he "thinks" or "feels" this god is like. The attributes of God in this sense are things man attributes to God. They do not really say anything about God *per se*. They only point to man's ideas about God. Thus modern theology either denies outright that God has any attributes or reduces them to some aspect of human psychology.

With its assumption that no objective revelation of the attributes of God exist, modern theologians are particularly hostile to the idea of God's having any "essential" attributes. If He did have "essential" attributes, this would limit man's freedom to mold God into whatever he pleased.

This would also make it impossible to view God as only a part of this world. Thus the idea of "essential" attributes is rejected.

Figure 10.1: Biblical Theology Verses Manmade Religion	
Biblical Theology	**Manmade Religion**
God ⟶ man	Man ⟶ god
revealed by God	created by man
objective	subjective
immutable	mutable
transcendent	cultural
absolute	relative
universal	contextual
knowledge	speculation
truth	myth

God's Essential Attributes

Why has historic Christian theology always believed that God has "essential" attributes? The only way we can distinguish one object from another is to identify those "attributes" or qualities that belong exclusively to one of the objects and without which the object cannot exist or be distinguished from anything else.

For example, how do we distinguish between a circle and a square? Can we draw a square circle or a circular square? No. The very attempt is absurd. It is obvious that a circle is not a square and a square is not a circle. But how do we *know* this? The essential "attribute" of a circle that makes a circle a "circle," and that no circle can exist without, in distinction from a square, is that the distance from the center of a circle to any point along its circumference will always be the same.

In the same way, God has "attributes" or qualities that make God GOD and without which He could not exist and could not be distinguished from anything else. These attributes cannot be applied to any other being. They belong only to God. Thus it is only by virtue of God's essential attributes that we can distinguish Him from the world and from the false gods of the heathen.

How do we identify the essential attributes of God? Christian theology has always taken the position that those attributes that are necessary for the existence of God and that describe His intrinsic nature or being are essential. Those attributes which refer to the works of God are not necessarily "essential."

For example, while the love of God is an essential attribute that makes God GOD, the act of sending His Son into the world was not "essential" or "necessary" for the existence or nature of God. He did not have to save anyone. He would still be GOD regardless if He threw everyone into the hell they so richly deserve.

It is in this sense that Christian theology has always viewed God's attributes of timelessness, omnipotence, omniscience, omnipresence, immutability, perfection, and sovereignty as "essential" attributes. To deny that God knows the future is to deny one of the essential attributes of God. To deny that God is timeless, immutable, or perfect is to deny that God is GOD.

The essential attributes of God are nonnegotiable. They all rise or fall together. In principle, if just one attribute is rejected, they must all be rejected. You can't have one without the others.

Questions for Discussion

1. Does God have attributes?
2. What do we mean when we say that God has "attributes?"
3. What is an "essential" attribute?
4. Where do man-made religions get their ideas of God?
5. Where do Christians get their ideas of God?

FOUR

MAKER OF HEAVEN
AND EARTH

What is truly wonderful is that Scripture not only teaches us that God has attributes, but it also tells us where to begin. The very first thing that God wants us to understand about Himself is that He is the Creator of heaven and earth. Thus the very first attribute is that God is the Creator.

> In the beginning, God created the heavens and the earth (Genesis 1:1).

The early Church understood this in a deeply profound way. They faced a pagan world that believed the universe was eternal and whatever gods existed were only finite parts of this world. Thus, according to the early Church, the first essential difference between the Christian God and the gods of the pagans was that He was the "Maker of Heaven and Earth."

In the theology, hymns, and creeds of the early Church, the doctrine of creation was viewed as the beginning point of all theology. All of the other attributes of God made sense only in the context of a God who existed prior to, independent of, and apart from the space-time universe that He created out of nothing for His own glory. If God is not the Creator, then He is not GOD. If someone accepts this fact, he will not have any problem with accepting anything else in Scripture.

The early Church was right in starting with the doctrine of creation, for it is the most mysterious and incomprehensible doctrine contained in the Bible. After all, what human mind can possibly fathom the act of Creation? Who can fully understand how God "spoke" the worlds into being? How did He bring everything out of nothing? How did He make life from nonlife? Why did He create angels and men, knowing that they would sin? Who can give a "coherent" explanation of Creation? Who can know the mind of the Creator and tell us the hows, whys, and wherefores of Creation?

We must bow in humility and awe before the God who is there in the very first sentence of His revelation. We must confess that creation out of nothing is beyond human reason and experience. This is why the author of Hebrews stated, "Faith is the conviction of things not seen" (Hebrews 11:1).

This is why the world focuses its main attack on the Biblical doctrine of creation. They revived the old Greek idea of evolution in order to cut the main taproot of Christianity. Once God is no longer viewed as the Creator of heaven and earth, then He is no longer the God who gives the world its existence. He becomes just one of many gods, all of whom derive their existence from the world!

The doctrine of creation is always the starting point throughout Scripture in any discussion of the "Gordian knots" of theology. Thus when Paul dealt with the issue of Divine sovereignty and man's moral accountability in Romans 9, he immediately turned the discussion to the doctrine of creation (vv. 20-21). When dealing with why wives are to submit to their husbands, he appealed to creation (1 Corinthians 11:7-9; 1 Timothy 2:12-13).

Is God the Author of Evil?

When dealing with the "problem of evil," the first step taken by Scripture is to affirm that "evil" is not eternal and thus it did not coexist with God as a rival god. The Zoroastrian idea of an eternal conflict between good and evil is refuted by the doctrine of creation. Evil is a finite part of the world God made.

But does this mean that God is the "author" of evil? If by "author" one asks if God is the "agent" of evil, the Biblical answer is no. When we sin, *we* do the sinning, not God. He does not *force* or *tempt* anyone into evil according to James 1:13-17. We sin because *we* choose to do so.

If by "author" one asks if God is "responsible" for evil, the answer is still no. The word *responsible* means accountability to a higher power to whom something is owed and who can demand payment of it. But there is no "higher power" to whom God is accountable. God is not accountable to anyone or anything outside Himself. God has no "Day of

Judgment." Whatever God does or says is always consistent with His own immutable nature.

If by the word *evil*, one means "an accident of chance or luck," the answer is no. There is no such thing as "luck" or "chance." Sin is not an "accident" that we can blame on God, the stars, the cards, or on Lady Luck. The concept of chance totally removes any human responsibility.

But while the Bible clearly teaches that God is not the "author of evil," at the same time, dozens of passages speak of God creating, sending, planning, and foreordaining evil! These passages are enough to show that while God is not the "author of evil" in the sense of being the agent of it, or of being accountable for it, yet, in some sense God "creates evil," "sends evil," "means it for good," etc. Surely these passages mean *something* and not nothing! (See: Isaiah 45:7; Amos 3:6; Job 2:10; Genesis 50:20; Deuteronomy 29:21; Joshua 23:15; Judges 2:15; Judges 9:23-24; 1 Samuel 18:10, 11; 1 Kings 9:9; 1 Kings 21:21, 29; 2 Kings 6:33; Exodus 4:11; 1 Samuel 2:6-7; Proverbs 16:4; Romans 11:36.)

Some theologians have tried to avoid the force of these and many other like passages by arguing that the "evil" spoken of is only "nonmoral evil." It is assumed that nonmoral evil is not *real* evil and hence not part of the issue of the problem of evil *per se*.

Several serious problems are found with this approach. First of all, the concept of nonmoral evil cannot be found anywhere in the text of Scripture. The Bible uses the same Hebrew and Greek words for "evil" whether speaking of sin or sickness. No exegetical basis for the distinction between moral and non-moral evil exists. The distinction between moral and nonmoral evil was a refinement of medieval theology and should not be arbitrarily read back into the text of Scripture.

The second problem with the idea of nonmoral evil is that this does not lessen the reality or gravity of the evils in view. Since the Bible calls all these things "evil," how these things are not *really* evil has yet to be explained.

We cannot imagine trying to comfort someone whose child was born blind by claiming that this was not a *real* evil, or, that the pain and suffering caused by a hurricane or an earthquake are not *really* evil.

While all evil is not sin *per se*, all evil comes from sin. For example, while sickness and death are not sins, they are "evils" that come from the Fall of man into sin (Romans 5:12).

Third, when the problem of evil is discussed, the kinds of evils that are raised as objections to God's foreknowledge, power, goodness, and existence are the *exact* evils mentioned in the texts. Anything that causes *pain* and *suffering* is assumed to be an "evil." Such things as disease, birth defects, blindness, lameness, ignorance, poverty, deception, war, and death are all considered as "evils."

The obvious solution is that what the Bible means by the word "evil" is not what pagan philosophers such as Epicurus meant. This never seems to occur to modern theologians. They assume the humanistic definitions of all the key terms used in the "problem of evil." Like Pavlov's dogs, whenever they see the word "evil" in the Bible, they yelp that it means "chance-produced evil." They never bother to exegete the text to see what the Bible means by such words.

Thus when they see the word *evil* in the above texts, this throws them into a state of confusion because God is pictured as *sending* evil upon people. In fact the Bible states many times that God *predestines* and *predetermines* evil. Evil is a part of His plan, called "His-story." Thus evil is not "chance-produced." It is *planned* by God Almighty!

Biblical Meaning of Evil

In the Bible, the different words for evil (Hebrew *ra*; Greek *kakos*, *poneros*) are used in the following ways:

1. The word *evil* is used as a description of the nature of man after the Adam's Fall. In Luke 11:13, Jesus describes man as "being evil." The present participle of the verb can be translated, "being and remaining evil."

2. Because man by nature is evil, all his thoughts, words, and deeds are called "evil" (Genesis 6:5; Mark 7:21-22; Romans 3:10-18).

3. The act of sin is "evil" (1 Kings 11:6).

4. Evil is not only the act of sin but also its resulting pain, suffering, or death. Thus evil can be the result of sin on one's self or the harm that one can do to others (2 Kings 22:16-17; Jonah 1:7).

5. God uses evil for His own purposes. (Genesis 50:20; Psalm 119:67, 71).

The fourth problem with the idea of nonmoral evil is the fact that such a concept does not solve the problem of evil. It is assumed that it is all right to say that God "creates," "plans," or "sends" *nonmoral* evil. Otherwise how can we explain the judgment of God on sinners? The plagues of Egypt are a good example of God's causing pain, suffering, and death. Hell, of course, is the greatest *evil* God ever created.

But when it comes to *moral* evil, it is claimed that we must never say that God "creates," "plans," or "sends" moral evil, for this would make God the "author" of evil.

The problem with this line of reasoning is that the Bible clearly speaks of evils that cannot be viewed as anything other than *moral* evils, and that God not only *foresaw* but also *planned* from all eternity! The greatest evil ever perpetrated in human history was the murder of the Son of God. Here we have a real moral evil. Does the Bible tell us that this evil was foreknown and foreordained by God, or does does it say that God did not know that Christ would die on the cross for our sins?

In terms of man's responsibility in the whole affair, Peter laid the entire evil on the shoulders of those who did it.

> *You* have taken and by *wicked* hands have crucified and slain (Acts 2:23).

The early Church agreed with this and saw Herod, Pontius Pilate, the Gentiles, and the Jews as the "author" of this, the greatest of all evils (Acts 4:27).

Yet, while man was "accountable" for this evil because he was the "agent" who did it freely and not under any external constraints, Peter and the early Church believed that this evil was foreknown, predestined, preordained, decreed, predetermined, and planned by God. Thus Peter said that Christ was:

> . . . delivered up *by the predetermined plan and foreknowledge of God* (Acts 2:23).

To this the Church agreed saying,

> For truly in this city there were gathered together against Thy holy Servant Jesus . . . both Herod and Pontius Pilate, along with the Gentile and the peoples of Israel, *to do whatever Thy hand and Thy purpose predestined to occur* (Acts 4:27-28).

How can we explain this seeming contradiction? Herod was responsible for doing something not only foreknown but also predetermined by Almighty God! The text cannot be any clearer.

There are only two possible ways of handling this. One way is to pretend that these passages do not exist. The tension is "solved" but at the expense of God's Word. This is what processian and moral government teachers do.

The second way is the historic Christian response, which is to bow before the mysteries of Revelation. When humanistic thinkers demand, "But *how* does God do this?" we respond that we don't know. All we know is what we have been told in Scripture. And Scripture tells us that God is "working all things together for our good" (Romans 8:28). This we believe although we cannot explain it.

Conclusion

Biblical Christians believe in God the Father Almighty, Maker of heaven and earth, and that everything that exists is part of the Creator's plan that will bring Him glory and honor both in this world and in the next.

Question for Discussion

1. What is the very first thing that God revealed about Himself to man?
2. With what doctrine does Christian theology begin?
3. Have you ever wondered about the problem of evil?
4. Is God the "author" of evil?
5. What is the biblical solution to the problem of evil?

FIVE

THE INCOMPREHEN-SIBILITY OF GOD

The God who has revealed Himself in Scripture tells us that He is going to be "incomprehensible" to us. But does this mean that God is going to be irrational or illogical? No. It means that God is *beyond* man's capacity to understand or explain exhaustively. In this sense, God is *beyond* human reason and logic because He is infinite and we are finite.

The doctrine of incomprehensibility is the opposite of rationalistic "reductionism," which reduces God to human categories in order to make Him "manageable," "coherent," and "explainable." Incomprehensibility allows God to be GOD. It reveals that God is infinitely better and greater than man. Thus we can build all the little theoretical molds we want, and we can try to force God into these molds, but in the end God will not "fit." He will always be *beyond* our grasp. He is too high for us to scale and too deep for us to fathom. We cannot get God in a box. The finite span of the human mind will never encompass the infinite God of Scripture.

But does this mean that God is "unknowable"? If by "unknowable" we mean the Greek philosophic dichotomy that "man must know either all or nothing," this is not what Christian theology means by its doctrine of incomprehensibility. We can have a true but finite knowledge of God on a personal and intellectual level because God has revealed Himself. Thus while we cannot fully understand the God who has revealed Himself, yet we can and do know Him. (See Jeremiah 9:23, 24; Daniel 11:32; John 17:3; Galatians 4:8-9; 1 John 4:4-8; 5:18-21.)

The doctrine of incomprehensibility means that we can only go so far and no further in our understanding of God because we are *limited* in three ways.

First, we are limited by the *finite capacity* of our minds. This is a "problem" that cannot be avoided any more than it can be overcome. So, we might as well as admit that we are not gods. Since we are finite creations of an infinite God, we will *never* understand it all.

Second, we are also limited by the *sinfulness* of our minds. Thus we have a *moral* problem as well as a capacity problem. By nature, we do not want the light of Truth. We prefer the darkness of error (Genesis 6:5; John 3:19-21). Sin and Satan have darkened and blinded our minds lest we see the Truth (Romans 1:28; 2 Corinthians 4:4). Only God's wondrous grace can overcome our moral aversion to truth and righteousness.

Third, we are limited by revelation. Paul warned the Corinthians "not to go beyond what is written" because it would lead to arrogance (1 Corinthians 4:6). The constraints of revelation are given in order to restrain man's depraved lust to make gods for himself. We are not free to speculate and come up with our own ideas of God. We are to study the Bible in order to learn *God's* ideas about Himself, to think God's thoughts after Him.

What are the consequences if we reject the doctrine of the incomprehensibility of God? While we might "cheer" at first because this gives a cheap and easy way to resolve the antinomies and paradoxes of Scriptures, it ultimately leads to a rationalistic denial of all Christian doctrine.

Stephen Davis is a good example of this process. He demands a "precise explanation" that is "coherent" to him, or he will not believe. In other words, if he cannot fully understand some aspect of the Christian God, he will throw it out because "man (in this case Davis) is the measure of all things." This is the basic assumption of secular and religious humanism.

Davis first applies his humanistic assumption to the issues of divine sovereignty and human accountability. He understands that the historic Christian solution beginning from the Apostolic Fathers is that *both* divine sovereignty and human accountability are true. Christians for two thousand years have also believed that no one is able to reconcile these two ideas. It is a Biblical mystery that demands faith, not explanation. Since those who hold to both doctrines at the same time openly admit that they cannot give a "precise explanation" of *how* divine sovereignty and human accountability are *both* true, Davis has no choice but to reject the Christian position that both are true. He must now choose one and reject the other.

But does he now choose God and exalt His glory? No, as a humanist, Davis will always exalt *man* at the expense of God. When the choice comes down to either God's being "free" to do as He pleases with what He made, or man's being "free" to do as he pleases, a humanist will always make man "free" and God "bound." Thus Davis argues;

> Take the person who tries to reconcile divine predestination of all events with human freedom by saying, "Well, I'm talking about a kind of predestination which allows for human freedom." Until it is explained precisely what this species of predestination is, we will be suspicious that the proposed reconciliation is spurious.[1]

While this is a quick and easy way of philosophically dismissing the position of the early Church and the Reformation, we should warn the reader that having established the *precedent* that "whatever cannot be precisely explained is spurious," Davis goes on to apply it to such doctrines as the indwelling of the Holy Spirit.

> Similarly, we would be suspicious of a person who tries to explain how an incorporate being can be spatially located somewhere by the use of what this person calls "an aspatial concept of inside of." Again, until it is explained precisely what this species of "inside of" is, we will reject the proposed reconciliation.[2]

Since no one can "precisely explain" *how* an "incorporate being," either the Holy Spirit or a demonic spirit, can exist "inside of" someone, Davis rejects the idea. He also calls into question the *omnipresence* of God, for who can "precisely explain" *how* God is everywhere present?[3] Davis concludes,

> If we want to be rational we have no choice but to reject what we judge to be incoherent.[4]

We had better consider the *way* that someone does theology because it sets a *precedent* that will be relentlessly applied to more and more Christian teaching until nothing is left. While a denial of predestination is exegetically foolhardy, it is not damnable. But it *is* damnable to deny the essential attributes of God, such as His omnipresence, or the doctrine of the indwelling of the Holy Spirit. Christians need to understand that they must first look at where a line of reasoning will take them before they unknowingly start down the "primrose path" to apostasy.

Let us now examine some of the Scriptures which clearly teach the doctrine of the incomprehensibility of God. We will begin with the book of Job as it contains the fullest treatment of the doctrine in the Bible.

The Book of Job

This book is the passage of full mention in the Bible concerning the problem of evil. And it is *also* the passage of full mention on the subject of the incomprehensibility of God. Thus any discussion of the problem of evil must involve an affirmation of the incomprehensibility of God.

In Job the problem of evil is "solved" by the doctrine of the incomprehensibility of God. In other words, Job's solution was to accept *both* that God is sovereign and that man is responsible. He did not try to explain this. He simply left such mysteries in the hands of God.

It is interesting to note that when we examined the books that claim to "solve" the problem of evil by reducing the power and knowledge of God, not one of them even mentioned the book of Job. Why is Job ignored? Perhaps they don't *like* the answer God gave Job out of the whirlwind, because this answer is the incomprehensibility of God.

Now, we must point out that the problem of evil was not an academic issue for Job. The pain and suffering caused by the death of his children, the theft of his goods, the loss of his health, the ruination of his marriage, and the criticism of his friends, were all real evils to him.

But when Job said that he was willing to receive "evil as well as good from God," he meant what he said (Job 2:10). He was even willing to worship the God who "took" away his children, wealth, and health, saying:

> The Lord gave and the Lord has taken away.
> Blessed be the name of the Lord (Job 1:21).

When his wife told him to curse God for all the evils He had sent their way, Job refused (Job 2:9). In the face of unbelievable pain and suffering, Job exclaimed,

> Though He slay me,
> I will hope in Him (Job 13:15).

This passage is very important, for in his mind, Job viewed God as his "Slayer." He did not say that "chance" or "bad luck" or even "the Devil" was the cause of all the evils which came upon him. He always assumed that God was in control of this world. Although the *agent* who *caused* the evil may have been the Devil, the Chaldeans, etc., Job bowed before God as the One who sent the evils his way. Yet, he did not "blame" or "curse" God as if He were the agent or cause of these evils.

Job held to two seemingly contradictory doctrines. On the one hand, God was not the author of evil in the sense of being its agent, and He was thus not accountable for it. Therefore God should not be cursed. On the other hand, God is sovereign and He sent all these evils on Job. Thus he states over and over again that it is *God* who "took" away his children, wealth, health, and happiness (Job 12:9). No other exegetical conclusion is possible. As we shall see, Job could live with two seemingly contradictory doctrines because he had a very deep belief in the incomprehensibility of God.

But *how* could he endure all these things and believe in God's sovereignty and not curse God? Why didn't he give up his belief in God and become an atheist? Why didn't he trade in his infinite God for a finite god like the gods of the heathen? They were "guilty but forgiven" because they were limited in power and could not know the future. Did Job ever limit his God in these ways? How did he handle it?

Job handled all the evils in life the same way true believers have always handled them. Faith! Mighty faith! Faith that looked to God alone! This was his secret.

Job ultimately accepted the fact that his "reason" was incapable of comprehending the Being and works of God. So, he simply trusted in God that He knew what He was doing. Job did not presume to instruct the Almighty or to be His counselor.

But Job and his friends had to learn the hard way to trust in God and not to lean on their own understanding. At the beginning they still tried to reason it out all by themselves. But after all their discussions, they never solved anything. The book of Job concludes with the solution that Divine revelation is the only way for man to find an answer. This is the enduring message of the Book of Job and God's eternal answer to the problem of evil.

Several passages in Job deserve close study.

> But as for me, I would seek God;
> And I would place my cause before God;
> Who does great and unsearchable things,
> Wonders without number (Job 5:9).

How does Job resolve the fact that God is good and, at the same time, that "He inflicts pain" (Job 5:18)? The answer given in Job 5:9 is that when we try to search out the whys and wherefores of God's actions, we will always find that His ways are "unsearchable," i.e., incomprehensible. His "wonders are without number" and cannot be counted and measured by man.

> Who does great things, unfathomable,
> And wondrous works without number.
> Were He to pass by me, I would not see Him;
> Were He to move past me, I would not perceive Him.
> Were He to snatch away, who could restrain Him?
> Who could say to Him, "What art Thou doing?" (Job 9:10-12)

Starting with the doctrine of Creation (v. 8), Job proceeds to the incomprehensible nature of God and His works. What God does is so "great" that no one can "fathom" its depths. This makes His works "wondrous" or "awe-inspiring."

Job now proceeds to the fact that we cannot "see" God. Thus we cannot "perceive" His motives or goals. Neither can we "restrain" Him from doing whatever He wants. Thus we have no right to challenge God by demanding, "What art Thou doing?"

> Can you discover the depths of God?
> Can you discover the limits of the Almighty?
> It is high as the heavens, what can you do?
> Its measure is longer than the earth,
> And broader than the sea.
> If He passes by or shuts up,
> Or calls an assembly, who can restrain Him?
> For He knows false men,
> And He sees iniquity without investigating (Job 11:7-11).

The impact of these rhetorical questions cannot be avoided. No one can "discover the depths of God" for the depths are bottomless. No one can "discover the limits of the Almighty" for He is limitless. The text states that even if we could search out all of creation in terms of its height, depth, length, and breadth, we still could not "discover," i.e., comprehend, the *infinite* nature of the Almighty.

This is also applied to the sovereign will of the Almighty. If He wants to "pass by or shut up" something (v. 10), no one can restrain Him. He will do as *He* pleases.

God's omniscience is then defined in terms of an *immediate* and *perfect* knowledge of all things including the sins of man (v. 11). God's knowledge does not "grow" because He does not have to investigate a matter to learn about it. No, God knows all things "without investigation," i.e., without waiting until the event and its investigation occurs. The incomprehensibility of God is the context for both God's sovereignty and God's omniscience.

> Then the Lord answered Job out of
>   the whirlwind and said,
> "Who is this that darkens counsel
> By words without knowledge?
> Now gird up your loins like a man,
> And I will ask you, and you instruct Me!
> Where were you when I laid the foundation of the earth!
> Tell Me, if you have understanding,
> Who set its measurements, since you know?" (Job 38:1-5)

Job and his friends had sat around discussing the problem of evil in terms of what had come upon Job. On the basis of human reason, they engaged in endless philosophical speculation and, in the end, failed to resolve anything. Although a great deal of heat was generated during their discussions, little light came of it.

At last, God gives a revelation to the problem of evil. The first thing that He does is to dismiss all the conclusions of human "reason" as "words without knowledge" that only "darken counsel." Paul echoes this thought when he states that the world with all its philosophical wisdom is sheer "foolishness" (1 Corinthians 1:18-21).

Then God challenges their ability and capacity to understand the questions and the answers to those questions. In fact, they had asked questions that were "too deep" for them. Not only did they not understand their questions, but even the answers were also beyond their capacity to understand. They were "in over their heads" and did not know it! This is why so many people drown in unbelief. And even when we toss out to them the lifeline of Scripture, they would rather drown in unbelief than accept God's revelation by faith. For four chapters, God challenges them,

So, you think that you are so smart that nothing is "beyond" you?
You don't even hesitate to tell Me how to run the universe I made!
Well, I have a few questions for you. We'll see if you are as smart as
you claim. Since you think that you can comprehend Me, let's see how
well you comprehend the world around you. After all, this should be
easy for you since you claim to understand Me!

God then proceeds to put Job and his friends in the "hot seat" and
give them "the third degree." Under divine interrogation, they soon realized that their "reason" and "intuition" were not sufficient. The sovereignty of God was the solution to the problem of evil.

> Then Job answered the Lord, and said,
> "I know that Thou canst do all things,
> And that no purpose of Thine can be thwarted.
> Therefore I have declared that which
> I did not understand.
> Things too wonderful for me,
>   which I did not know.
> Hear, now, and I will speak;
> I will ask You, and You instruct me.
> Therefore I retract,
> And I repent in dust and ashes" (Job 42:1-4, 6).

Under the rebuke of God for trying by "reason" to solve the problem
of evil, Job "repents" and "retracts" all the things he and his friends had
said. He now bows before revelation and submits to the Divine glory.
He admits that God can do whatever He wants and no one can frustrate
or condemn His sovereign will. He admits that such questions are "too
wonderful," i.e., mysterious, for him. He will leave such things to God.

Other Passages

The rest of Scripture follows Job in resolving the problem of evil by
submitting to the incomprehensibility of God. Let us examine a few of
these passages.

> Such knowledge is too wonderful for me;
> It is too high, I cannot attain to it (Psalm 139:6).

In this Psalm, David first introduces the subject of God's omniscience in verses 1-5, which leads him to the incomprehensibility of God in verse 6. Then he goes on to describe the omnipresence of God in verses 7-12. David did not become depressed over the fact that God's omniscience and omnipresence are concepts that were "too high" for him to comprehend. The opposite was true. The incomprehensibility of God enhanced his worship. He could worship such a God because He is so *wonderful.*

> Great is the Lord, and highly to be praised;
> And His greatness is unsearchable (Psalm 145:3).

In the context, David has in mind not only the "greatness" of God's being, but also of His works. The word "unsearchable" is often translated "unfathomable." A nautical term, it meant that the plumb line of human reason will never discover a bottom to God in His nature or deeds. The true God has no "bottom" or limit for man to discover. Such a God is alone worthy of our worship.

> Why do you say, O Jacob, and assert, O Israel,
> "My way is hidden from the Lord
> And the justice due me escapes the notice of my God"?
> Do you not know? Have You not heard?
> The everlasting God, the Lord, the Creator of the
> ends of the earth,
> Does not become weary or tired.
> His understanding is inscrutable (Isaiah 40:27-28).

The apostate among Israel cherished two vain hopes. First, they hoped that God was limited in His knowledge and thus did not know about their sin. If He did not know about it, they would not get punished for it.

Second, they hoped that if God were not ignorant, at least He would be distracted by far more important things than meting out the justice due to them. If He were going to punish anyone, He would have to begin with people who are really wicked, not them. Or, perhaps, He was just uninterested in them and wouldn't care.

The prophet Isaiah dashes to the ground all such finite views of God that would see Him as "growing" or "learning." God is not ignorant, distracted, or uninterested, because the eternal God is the Creator of all things including man. His "understanding" or "knowledge" is not limited in any way by what He has made. It is thus "inscrutable," i.e., unlimited.

> Oh the depths of the riches both of the wisdom
>   and knowledge of God!
> How unsearchable are His judgments
>   and unfathomable His ways!
> For who has known the mind of the Lord,
> Or who became His counselor?
> Or who has first given to Him
>   that it might be paid back to him again?
> For from Him and through Him and to Him
>   are all things.
> To Him be the glory forever. Amen (Romans 11:33-36).

This is one of the most beautiful statements on the incomprehensibility of God in the New Testament. It is brought in by the Apostle Paul as the doxological climax to his discussion of election, predestination, God's sovereignty, and human responsibility in Romans 8-11. The Apostle Paul calls us to worship a God who is *beyond* our capacity to comprehend in either His being or works. This God is "unsearchable" and "unfathomable." No one will ever "know" all the "ins and outs" of the mind of the Lord. If someone could, he would "become His counselor," for he who can understand God would be greater than God.

The immediate occasion of this doxology to the incomprehensible God is his discussion of the inclusion of the Gentiles into the covenant of grace and the exclusion of Israel. Paul states that God's election is based on His grace and not on some condition of man such as race or parentage (Romans 11:.6-7).

But what about all the "whys," "hows," and "wherefores" that naturally arise? Paul does not claim to know all the answers. He knows only what has been revealed. Thus he can now freely worship God because he leaves such mysteries in the hands of his Creator:

> The love of Christ which surpasses knowledge (Ephesians 3:19).

Paul prays that the saints might "comprehend" and "know" the love of Christ (vv. 18-19). But while they can have a finite but true knowledge of such things, they cannot exhaustively comprehend the Lord Jesus Christ or His love. Christ is God as well as man. He is infinite in His being and love. We will never be able to understand the "whys," "hows," and "wherefores" of His love for sinners.

Let us point out that if we begin with the rationalistic assumption that everything must either be "precisely explained" or we must reject it, then we must reject the love of Christ because it "surpasses comprehension." God's election and love are so joined in Scripture that they either stand or fall together.

The peace of God which surpasses all comprehension (Philippians 4:7).

Who can "precisely explain" *how* the peace of God can "indwell" us and gives us comfort? Who can make "coherent" the ways of the Spirit of God? Is not the work of God in the soul like the wind which comes and goes without our permission or knowledge (John 3:8)?

If we are limited to what can be "precisely explained" and "made coherent," then we will have to reject the peace of God as well as the love of Christ! But if we accept the incomprehensibility of God, we can have both His peace and His love. By this faith we can live without fear, being confident in His sovereign love and power.

Conclusion

From just these few passages of Scripture it is abundantly clear that the Christian doctrine of the incomprehensibility of God is a revealed truth. It follows naturally after the doctrine of creation and forms the context of all the other attributes of God.

It is also clear that the authors of Scripture were not embarrassed by the incomprehensibility of God but proud of it. They did not apologize for it but boasted of it. They did not agonize over it but rejoiced in it. They were not driven away from God by it but were drawn nigh unto God because of it. They did not curse God but fell at His feet in wonder, awe, and praise.

Questions for Discussion

1. Is God greater than our minds can grasp?
2. Where is the "passage of full mention" in the Bible which deals with the incomprehensibility of God?
3. What does this doctrine mean to you?

SIX

THE INCOMPARA- BILITY OF GOD

The God of the prophets and apostles is so wonderful in all His being and attributes that He cannot be reduced to the level of the pagan gods or man. God simply cannot be "compared" to the gods or man as if they were His equals. What the gods are like has *no* bearing whatsoever on the God who is there and who has revealed Himself in Scripture.

The incomparability of God has always been denied by humanistic thinkers because they think God is no "better" or "greater" than themselves. They assume God must be "like" the other gods and "like" man himself. This leads to a theology in which the nature of God is determined by looking at the gods of the heathen and at man himself. Whatever limitations man has, God is said to have, because He is "just like us."

Pagan thinkers always argue from what *they* can or cannot do to what God can or cannot do. Since *they* cannot know the future, then God cannot know it either. Since *they* cannot rule the world, then neither can God. Since *they* have to learn things by trial and error, then God must do likewise. Since *they* have to wait around until things happen before they can know them, then so must God. Since *their* understanding is finite and *their* power is limited, then so is God's. Since *they* are neither perfect nor immutable, then God is neither perfect nor immutable. In short, *they* create God in *their* own image and likeness!

But God has revealed that He is *not* like man or his false gods. Thus God cannot be compared to them, for He is "better" in quality by being Divine and "greater" in quantity by being Infinite. This is one of the *major* Biblical themes of God's glory.

The following texts will demonstrate two things. First, the very "Godhood" of God is involved in His incomparability. God is GOD because He is *not* like man or his gods. Second, God is not like man or his gods because of those very attributes of God which pagan thought has always rejected. God is the incomparable GOD because He is the Creator, the sovereign Lord of all things, and the omniscient One who foreknows the future!

> Who is like Thee among the gods, O Lord?
> Who is like Thee, majestic in holiness,
> Awesome in praises, working wonders (Exodus 15:11)?

Miriam's song of triumph after Pharaoh's army perished in the Sea magnifies the sovereign power of God. Which of the finite pagan gods can do what Yahweh has done? He is incomparable in His character and power.

> There is none like the God of Jeshurun . . .
> The eternal God is a dwelling place,
> And underneath are the everlasting arms . . .
> So Israel dwells in security (Deuteronomy 33:26-28).

In Moses' farewell blessing, he blesses Asher by teaching him the incomparability of Yahweh. He alone is the "eternal God" who transcends space and time. His sovereign power, or "everlasting arms," is the only basis of security for God's people.

> My soul shall rejoice in the Lord;
> It shall exalt in His salvation.
> All my bones will say, "Lord, who is like Thee,
> Who delivers the afflicted
>   from him who is too strong for him" (Psalm 35:9-10).

As David sees his enemies approaching with a force too great for him to overcome, he cries out to God for deliverance. In his prayer he reminds the Lord that He is incomparable in His mercy as well as in His judgment.

> But to the wicked God says,
> You thought that I was just like you;

I will reprove you (Psalm 50:16, 21).

God begins His address to the wicked in verse 16. They are condemned because they hypocritically speak of God's statutes and covenant while rejecting God's revelation! But their greatest crime is their wicked assumption that God is limited just like them. They are able to abandon themselves to sin because they think that God is limited in knowledge and does not know what they are doing, and that God is limited in power and cannot do anything about it anyway. God is going to "tear them into pieces" because they have "forgotten" what God is really like (v. 22). Humanists always assume God is "just like man."

> For Thy righteousness, O God,
>   reaches to the heavens;
> Thou who hast done great things;
> O God, who is like Thee? (Psalm 71:19)

In the context, the Psalmist focuses on the "righteousness," i.e. justice, of God because it "reaches to the heavens," i.e., is infinite. This infinite justice of God is declared to be incomparable and becomes the basis of his hope that God will deliver him from his enemies.

> There is no one like Thee among the gods, O Lord;
> Nor are there any works like Thine.
> For Thou art great and doest wondrous deeds;
> Thou alone art God (Psalm 86:8, 10).

David cries out for deliverance to a sovereign God who is "great" in His being and works. God's sovereignty is so complete and universal that even David's enemies are under the control of God! David's enemies can "choose" to do him harm, but God is in control and will deliver His people.

> The Lord is high above all nations;
> His glory is above the heavens.
> Who is like the Lord our God,
> Who is enthroned on High,
> Who humbles Himself to behold
> The things that are in heaven and in the earth (Psalm 113:4-6)?

The Psalmist begins in awe with a vision of the transcendence of God over man ("the nations") and nature ("heavens and earth.") This transcendent God is sovereign over all things for He is "enthroned on high." He is called "the Most High God" no fewer than forty-six times in Scripture.

But does this mean that He is not immanent "in" the world because He is transcendent "above" it? No, the Psalmist believes that God is *both* transcendent and immanent. The Lord "humbles Himself to behold" all that takes place in heaven and in the earth.

The Psalmist thus concludes that God is incomparable because He is transcendent, sovereign, and omniscient. The gods of the heathen are *not* transcendent, sovereign, or omniscient. They are "of" the world as well as "in" the world. But the True God is "above" the world (transcendent), "over" the world (sovereign), "in" the world (immanent), and knows all "about" the world (omniscient). God is GOD because of these things.

> To whom then will you liken God?
> Or what likeness will you compare with Him (Isaiah 40:18)?

Isaiah 40 is the passage of full mention on subject of the transcendence of God. He is depicted as the sovereign Creator and Ruler of the universe, who sits enthroned far above all earthly powers. The nations are only "a drop in a bucket" or "a speck of dust on the scales" (v. 15). All the inhabitants of the earth are "like grasshoppers" (v. 22).

Thus it is absurd to make an idol and compare it to God (v.18). What is an idol but a manmade god (vv. 19f.). How can such ignorant gods compare to the True God, who is omniscient (vv.13-14)?

> To whom then will you liken Me?
> That I should be his equal?" says the Holy One.
> Lift up your eyes on high
> And see who has created these stars,
> The One who leads forth their hosts by number
> He calls them all by name;
> Because of the greatness of His might and the
>   strength of His power
> Not one of them is missing (Isaiah 40:25-26).

God is not only incomparable because He is transcendent and omniscient, but also because He is omnipotent. His omnipotence is revealed in creation and providence. He created the stars. This shows His omnipotence. He knows them all by name which reveals His omniscience. And His power sustains them in their orbits, which reveals His Providence. The gods of the heathen are limited in power and knowledge. The God of Israel should not be compared to these idols.

> I am the first and I am the last,
> And there is no God besides Me.
> And who is like Me? Let him proclaim and declare it;
> Yes, let him recount it to Me in order,
> From the time that I established the ancient nation.
> And let them declare to them
>   the things that are coming
> And the events that are going
>   to take place (Isaiah 44:6-7).

Isaiah now bases the incomparability of God on His eternity. As "the First and the Last," God is transcendent over time itself. Thus he appeals to God's absolute and infallible foreknowledge of the future as proof of His uniqueness. Which of the gods of the heathen can "recount" history from "the beginning to the end"? Which of them can tell us future events? Only the true God can do this.

> I am God, and there is no one like Me,
> Declaring the end from the beginning
> And from ancient times
>   things which have not been done,
> Saying, "My purpose will be established,
> And I will accomplish
>   all My good pleasure" (Isaiah 46:9-10).

No wonder pagan philosophers have always attacked God's foreknowledge and foreordination of the future! Since Isaiah records God's claim that He is GOD because He foreknows and ordains the future, the heathen have always made their chief attack on those very attributes. Once God is denied knowledge and control of the future, then He is "just like" their gods.

"For my thoughts are not your thoughts,
Neither are your ways My ways," declares the Lord.
"For as the heavens are higher than the earth,
So are My ways higher than your ways,
And My thoughts than your thoughts" (Isaiah 55:8-9).

Isaiah now tells us that God's thoughts and ways cannot be compared to man's thoughts and ways. The limitations of man's thoughts and ways should not be placed on God. Man is *not* the measure of all things. God is His own interpreter and He has made it plain that He is *not* a man and should not be limited in power and knowledge as if He were a man (Numbers 23:19; Hosea 11:9).

Humanistic theologians are forever trying to instruct God as to what He may and may not do. They try to inform the Holy One about what is just and unjust. They are cosmic "back-seat drivers" who gripe and complain about the direction in which history is going, and who then take it upon themselves to tell the Almighty how to run the world He made for His own glory! Their conceit and imprudence know no bounds!

There is none like Thee, O Lord;
Thou art great, and great is Thy name in might.
Who would not fear Thee, O King of the nations?
Indeed it is thy due!
For among all the wise men of the nations,
And in all their kingdoms,
There is none like Thee . . .
But the Lord is the true God;
He is the living God and the everlasting King . . .
Thus you shall say to them,
"The gods that did not make the heavens
    and the earth shall perish
    from the earth and from under the heavens."
It is He who made the earth by His power,
Who established the world by His wisdom;
And by His understanding
    He has stretched out the heavens . . .
Every man is stupid, devoid of knowledge;
Every goldsmith is put to shame by his idols;
For his molten images are deceitful,
And there is no breath in them . . .

The Portion of Jacob is not like these;
For the Maker of all is He,
And Israel is the tribe of His inheritance,
The Lord of hosts is His name (Jeremiah 10:6-16).

The true God cannot be compared to such absurdities. He is the omnipotent Maker and Sustainer of all things. All attempts to lower God down to the level of the finite gods of the heathen are sheer "stupidity," says Isaiah.

Conclusion

These Biblical passages are clear enough to establish the doctrine of the incomparability of God. Why then should we follow the processians in rejecting those very attributes of God which make Him different from and superior to the gods of the heathen? Why reduce God to the level of pagan deities by claiming that He cannot know or control the future? If God is no better or greater than man or his manmade gods, why believe or worship Him? Are we really any better off if God is no longer GOD?

Such searching questions as these can be ignored only at the peril of one's immortal soul. Theology is not a game but a matter of eternal life or death. If you want a finite god, then you must choose Baal and serve him. But if you want to serve Jehovah, then you must accept Him as He has revealed Himself in the Bible: the omnipotent, omniscient, sovereign Creator and Sustainer of heaven and earth.

Questions for Discussion

1. Is the Christian's God like the gods of other religions?
2. Do all religions worship the same God — just under different names?
3. What makes the biblical God unique?

SEVEN

THE UNITY OF GOD

*T*he pagan doctrine of polytheism can be successfully refuted by the Christian doctrine of the unity of God. The "unity" or "oneness" of God teaches us several different things about God.

First, the True God is ONE in *number*. There never were, are not now, and never shall be any other true gods. That this is the clear teaching of Scripture cannot be denied. (See 1 Kings 8:60; Isaiah 43:10; 44:6,8; 45:5, 18, 21, 22; 46:9; Jeremiah 10:10; John 17:3; 1 Corinthians 8:4, 6; 1 Thessalonians 1:9; 1 Timothy 2:5.)

Second, God is ONE in *nature*. He is a divine being and not just a random collection of independent attributes. This means that we cannot simply "pay our nickel and take our choice" when it comes to the attributes of God. The attributes of God are so interrelated that one cannot be rejected without rejecting all of them. The attributes are defined in terms of each other. They modify one another and form the context of their mutual understanding. They stand or fall together. Thus the unity of God means that we must accept *all* of God as He has revealed Himself in Scripture. We cannot "cut" God into pieces.

Processians are in the nasty habit of thinking that they can pick and choose among the attributes and still end up with the Christian God. They assume that they can reject some attributes of God and this will not affect the remaining attributes. But when anyone tries surgically to remove any of the essential attributes of God, the patient dies just as surely as when someones has his heart, lungs, and brain removed!

When a moral government teacher denies the sovereignty, foreknowledge, perfection, immutability, and omnipotence of God, the remaining

ing product is only a god and not God at all because all the attributes have been radically altered.

For example, processians "like" the attribute of the love of God. We are not aware of any of them that throw it out, even though Scripture describes it as "beyond understanding." But they "dislike" the sovereignty of God as much as they like His love. So, while they gladly accept the love of God, they throw out His sovereignty.

The only "fly in the ointment" is the exegetical fact that the only "love" of God spoken of in Scripture is a *sovereign* love. God's love is never described in the Bible as a weak pathetic sentimentalism. God is not wringing his hands and whining that he "loves" man but can't "interfere" because of man's "free will."

If we take the Bible seriously, the love of God for His people is sovereign and it led Him to predestine them to adoption as sons before the world was created (Romans 8:28-30; Ephesians 1:4, 5, 11). He sovereignly "draws them" to Himself (Jeremiah 31:3; Psalm 65:4; John 6:44), sovereignly "opens" their hearts (Acts 16:14), and sovereignly gives them the gifts of repentance and faith (Acts 11:18; Philippians 1:29).

But we cannot stop here. The processians also deny the immutability and perfection of God. This means that God's love can no longer be understood as changeless or perfect. God's love becomes fickle, defective and hence unreliable. This stands in dark contrast to the love of God spoken of in Scripture, which is both immutable and perfect!

The Bible and the Gods

Third, the Bible uses the word "Elohim" (gods) in a figurative and symbolic way to refer to men and angels when they carry out a God-like function. Moses (Exodus 4:16) and the judges of Israel (Exodus 21:6; 22:8, 9; Psalm 82:6) are called "gods" because, like God, they held the power of life and death over men.

While the idols of the heathen are also called "gods" (1 Corinthians 8:5), the authors of Scripture are careful to state that they were "false gods" and that there is actually only one God "by nature" (1 Corinthians 8:6; Galatians 4:8).

The figurative use of the word "gods" in the Bible should not be confused with polytheism, which is the belief in many gods. In John 10:30-36, when Jesus quoted Psalm 82:6 to the Jews who were about to stone Him, He was not saying that his enemeies were "gods" in the sense of real deity. He was not saying that we should pray to or worship them.

What He was doing was answering their objection to His claim of deity in verse 30. How could they get so mad at Him for claiming to be "God" when the word *Elohim* was at times even used of mere men such as the judges of Israel? He was greater than they because He was one in nature with the Father. The Jews got the point and picked up stones, saying, "You being a man, make yourself out to be God" (John 10:33). They knew He was not just claiming to be "a god" in a figurative sense like the judges of Israel. He was claiming to be the one true GOD! This is why they screamed, "Blasphemy!"

The Bible has some very harsh things to say about the gods of the heathen. Their "gods" are not "true" or "real" but only "nonexistent" fictions. The idols that represent them are only wood, stone, or metal. They are "nothing" because they are "lifeless." They are thus "profitless," "speechless," and "powerless." They are "dumb idols" which only "stupid" people worship. When an idol is worshiped, this worship goes to demons, not God. (See 1 Chronicles 16:26, cf. Psalm 96:5; 2 Kings 19:18, cf. Isaiah 37:19; 2 Chronicles 13:9; Jeremiah 2:11; 5:7; 10:8-10; 16:20; Habakkuk 2:18-20; Acts 19:26; 1 Corinthians 8:4-5; 10:20; Galatians 4:8.)

It is interesting to note that in the passages above, the gods were not true deity because they could not know or foretell the future.

Conclusion

There is but one true eternal Triune God of Father, Son, and Holy Spirit. He alone is worthy of our worship and praise.

Questions for Discussion

1. Is there only one God or are there many?
2. Does the Bible deny the existence of the gods of heathen religion?
3. Can we pick and choose when it comes to the attributes of God?
4. Are the attributes so interrelated that if you deny one you have in effect denied them all?

EIGHT

THE SELF-EXISTENCE OF GOD

The Scriptures reveal an eternal, transcendent God who existed prior to, independent of, and apart from the universe He created out of nothing for His own glory. This is in direct conflict with the processian heresy of a "dipolar deity" in which God is as dependent on the world for His existence as the world is dependent upon God.

The historic Christian position is that God's existence is:

- real and not mythological
- eternal and not temporal
- independent and not dependent
- infinite and not finite
- perfect and not imperfect
- absolute and not relative
- immutable and not mutable

God is the "self-existent" One because God "has life in Himself" and not in some "ground of being" outside of Himself (John 5:26). He is not dependent on space or time for His existence because He pre-existed them and they were created out of nothing.

The attribute of self-existence is directly involved with the issue of whether God is "timeless." Is God "in" time and, therefore, dependent on TIME for His own existence? Or is time "in" God and dependent on GOD for its existence? Who is the ultimate "ground of being"? Is Time the GOD of God?

It is claimed by processians that God is as dependent on time as man is because time is as eternal as God. Thus God exists "in" time like man. Time is the ultimate "ground of being," not God. God is thus a dependent being like man and the gods of the heathen.

The Christian Church has always taught that God is timeless for two reasons. First, God is the only *eternal* Being and nothing is eternal along side of, beneath, or over God. If time were eternal, then it would be a rival god or a higher god upon whom God depended for His existence. Second, God created the space-time universe out of nothing. God is not dependent on the space-time world for His existence, for He existed prior to it. He does not depend on time or space for He is GOD.

As we have already seen, the attributes of God stand or fall together. If we deny that God knows or controls the future, we have to tamper with all of the other attributes until nothing of GOD is left. If God's timelessness is denied, He is no longer the living God of Scripture.

That this is the clear teaching of Scripture can be seen from the following passages.

The Living God

God is described as the "living God" thirty times in Scripture, with the New Testament using the phrase at least fifteen times. The "living God" is often contrasted to the "lifeless" gods of the heathen who were dependent upon time and space for their existence. (See Deuteronomy 5:26; Joshua 3:10; 1 Samuel 17:26; Psalm 42:2; Isaiah 37:4; Jeremiah 10:10; Matthew 16:16; Acts 14:15; 1 Thessalonians 1:9.)

In Exodus 3:14, we are told that God's name is "I AM." This word in the original means that He is the eternally existent One who always was, is, and shall be the same throughout all eternity. He is the Eternal I AM.

It is thought by many that the book of Job was the first book of the Bible ever written. Thus it is the earliest record of God's self-revelation in Scripture. In Job, God is described as the One:

> In whose hand is the life of every living thing, and the breath of all mankind (Job 12:10).

In Job 33:4, Job tells us that:

> The Spirit of God has made me, and the breath of the Almighty gives me life.

Job did not think that God was receiving His life, i.e., His existence, from time or anything else. God was the GIVER and not the receiver of life.

When Daniel rebuked Belshazzar and foretold his doom and the destruction of his kingdom, he not only revealed that God knows all about the future, but he also instructed him concerning the true nature of God.

> You have praised the gods of silver and gold, of bronze, iron, wood, and stone, which do not see, hear, or understand. But the God in whose hand are your life-breath and your ways, you have not glorified (Daniel 5:23).

Belshazzar made a big mistake when he assumed that he was "free" from God. His life's breath was in the hands of the Almighty who was the Creator and Sustainer of all things.

The Apostle Paul in his address to the Greeks on Mars Hill was careful to point out that the God whom he represented was self-existent. He was not dependent like their gods. He was the One upon whom all things depended for their existence.

> The God who made the world and all things in it, since He is Lord of heaven and earth, does not dwell in temples made with hands; neither is He served by human hands, as though He needed anything, since He Himself gives to all life and breath and all things; . . . for in Him we live and move and exist (Acts 17:24, 25, 28).

Here Paul teaches that God's existence is *independent* and does not rely on anything outside Himself. It is *perfect* and is not lacking in anything. And it is *immutable* and *absolute*, for all things including time and space depend upon Him. God does not "need" time or anything else for His existence.

Conclusion

But how is God's "self-existence" possible? Can we give a "precise" and "coherent" explanation of God's self-existence? Can anyone fully understand how He has "life in Himself?" No! Does this bother us? No! Why?

Without faith it is impossible to please Him, for he who comes to God must *believe that He is*, and that He is a rewarder of those who seek Him (Hebrews 11:6, italics mine).

Questions for Discussion

1. What do we ment when we say that God "exists?"
2. Does God depend on something or someone else for His own existence?
3. Can God be GOD if He is dependent on Time for His existence?
4. Where does the Bible teach the self-existence of God?

NINE

INVISIBLE AND INCORPOREAL

According to Jesus, God is *spirit* in His essence or nature (John 4:24) and a "spirit" by definition does not have a physical body (Luke 24:39). Thus we should not think of God as the "Man Upstairs," because He does not have a male human body. "God is not a man" (Numbers 23:19).

Since God is spirit, He is invisible (Colossians 1:15; 1 Timothy 1:17; Hebrews 11:27). Thus, no one has seen God the Father, for there is nothing physical to see (John 1:18). The only way to see God is to see Him in His Son, who became a real man of flesh and blood (John 1:14-18; 14:9).

In John 4:24, Jesus did not say that "God is *a* spirit" but "God is spirit." The distinction is crucial. If God were "a spirit" this would imply that He is only one *finite* spirit among many others. He would be in essence no different from the Devil and his demons. But when Jesus said that God was "spirit," this implied that He is spirit in an *infinite* sense. God cannot have a body because He is infinite spirit. Those who deny God's infinite nature are actually robbing God of His spirituality.

This also applies directly to the issue of whether God is "timeless." If God is not timeless and spaceless but "in" time and space like man, then God's being is reduced to some kind of "matter" or "form" and must "struggle to overcome" such problems as gravity, the speed of light, entropy, and inertia. This was clearly believed by Whitehead and most processians.

Christians have always believed that time and space are attributes of created things, not of the Creator. Thus God is described as the "eternal Spirit" in Hebrews 9:14. God is not only spaceless but also timeless.

One error is consistently made by processians at this point. When the creeds of the early Church stated that God did not have a body and thus He did not have "parts or passions," some processians have twisted this to mean that the God of historic Christian theism is devoid of any "emotions." This is labeled as a "Platonic" element in Christian theology. Such a God does not "love" or "hate" because He has no "passions." Thus the historic Christian concept of God is defective. Clark Pinnock, for instance, gives this kind of argument.[1]

In reality, when the early Fathers and such creeds as the Westminster Confession of Faith state that God does not have any "passions," this has reference to God's not having any *bodily* passions. For example, since God does not have a stomach, He has no "passion" for food. Since God has no reproductive organs, He has no sexual "passions." This was said to distinguish God from the gods of the heathen who ate, drank, raped, and plundered. The charge that the creeds of the Church deny that God has emotions is absurd.

Conclusion

In His nature, God is both eternal and infinite in spirit and cannot be reduced to a finite time-bound being who struggles with a chance-directed universe. God is not a man.

Questions for Discussion

1. Why is God invisible?
2. What do you think about such cults as the Mormons who teach that God is a man?
3. Can God be everywhere at the same time if He corporate?

TEN

PERSONAL AND INFINITE

Christian theology has very carefully stated that while God is infinite and spiritual in His essence, this does not mean that He is an impersonal "it." The Greeks had fallen into the trap of assuming that God must be either finite and personal or infinite and nonpersonal. But this dichotomy is never found in the Bible.

God is "personal" in that He is a self-conscious ego who can say, "I AM" (Exodus 3:14). He has intellect (Romans 11:34), thoughts (Isaiah 58:8-9), will (Romans 12:2), emotion (John 3:16), and action (Ephesians 1:11). He cannot be reduced to a nonpersonal "ground," "force," or "energy." An "I AM" is far superior to an "it."

Some processians have argued that God "needs" the world to fulfill Himself. Since this "need" of God would be eternal, the world must be eternal. The doctrine of creation is thus rejected because God needs the world for His own growth and knowledge. It is by this assumption that they made time eternal, holding that God "needs" time to exist.

The historic Christian response to such pagan ideas is to point out that God is a Trinity: God the Father, God the Son, and God the Holy Spirit. Because the fellowship and communication within the Three Persons of the Trinity is both eternal and self-sufficient, God is not "lonely." He does not "need" man or the space/time world. The Father, the Son, and the Holy Spirit have gotten along just fine for all eternity without man or the world.

Only the infinite God of the Bible can give man a sufficient basis for universal truths and moral absolutes. Being infinite in nature, God, not man, is the "measure of all things." God, not man, is the Origin and

Judge of truth and morals. God, not man, is the infinite reference point by which all the particulars of life can find their meaning.

Infinitude and Ignorance Do Not Mix

Now you would think that "evangelicals" would be the last ones to deny the infinitude of God. But this is what "evangelical" processians and "Arminian" moral government people do when they deny God's omnipotence, omniscience, immutability, sovereignty, and perfection. Why? The word "infinite" means *unlimited*. Thus when God's knowledge and power are *limited* by claiming that He cannot know or control the future, then God is no longer unlimited, i.e., *infinite*.

While the philosophically astute "evangelical" processians understand this, some of the moral government people, having no background in philosophy or logic, have naively assumed that God is still infinite, i.e. "unlimited," even though they have limited most of His attributes! This is totally irrational. To say that God is limited and unlimited at the same time is like trying to draw a square circle!

Once we deny any of the infinite attributes of God, He becomes a *finite* being. Once this happens, God can no longer be the Origin of universal truths and moral absolutes. Why? A finite god needs an infinite reference point to explain him! God becomes just one more particular in search of a universal! Everything becomes "relative," including God.

For example, if god does not know the future, then his present knowledge is *limited*. Since his present knowledge is limited, it becomes mutable, imperfect, and relative. What he knows *today* is incomplete and may need readjustment *tomorrow*. It may even be wrong because he did not have at that time all the information he needed. Thus whatever a finite god says today must be taken with a grain of salt because his understanding of the situation is as limited as man's understanding. Since a finite god cannot see the future, he cannot see the "big picture."

The modern attack on God's infinite nature is a master stroke of Satan. If he can get people to deny just *one* attribute of God, he has destroyed *all* the infinite attributes of God in one swoop.

The word "infinite" as used in Christian theology is not an independent attribute. It is actually an adjective, that when applied to all the other attributes, makes God GOD. In other words, it is the addition of the concept of "infinity" that makes God the Creator instead of a creature.

For example, what is the *difference* between the person and presence of angels and men as opposed to the person and presence of God? While the person and presence of angels and men are both *finite* in that they are *limited* to being only in one place at one time, God's person and presence are both *infinite* in that He is *unlimited* and thus everywhere present in the totality of His person. God is omnipresent only by virtue of the fact that He is infinite!

God's knowledge is *different* from the knowledge of angels and men because it is infinite, i.e., omniscient. His power is *different* because it is infinite, i.e., omnipotent. And even His moral attributes of love, mercy, grace, goodness, and holiness are *different* from angels and men because they are infinite, i.e., without end or limitation.

This leads us to ask what it would mean if we deny that God's attributes are infinite, i.e., unending and inexhaustible? This would mean that the love and mercy of God are limited! The day may come when we ask forgiveness from God and He must say, "Sorry, I can't help you. I don't have any left. I'm only finite, you know."

Not only is the concept of "infinite" the only way we have to show how God is *different* from His creation, but it also reveals how God is *superior*. God's "infinity" should not be reduced to the mathematical idea of a "boundless quantity." While God is *quantitatively* distinct from His creation by being "infinite," i.e., not limited like the things He made, infinitude also means a *perfection* of God whereby He is *superior* to what He has made in a *qualitative* sense. Thus God's infinite presence or omnipresence is *superior* to the finite presence of men and angels. God's infinitude is a quality of perfection that makes all His attributes superior as well as different to those of angels and men.

God is GOD because He is different in a superior way to the world both quantitatively and qualitatively. God cannot be limited, exhausted, or quantified. His person, presence, power, prescience, knowledge, moral qualities, or glory have no end, boundary, or limitation. No one will ever find a "cut-off point" for God. We can never draw a line and then tell God that He can only go so far and no further. This is what Christians mean when they say that God is "infinite."

The Evidence for God's Infinitude

The evidence for the infinite nature of God rests on the clear Biblical teaching that He is the Creator of all things. When God created the world, His power was not exhausted or depleted by the act of creation because His power is infinite. But the limited power of a finite god would have been exhausted. The idea of a "tired" god who is too worn out and weak to do anything sounds more like Zeus than Jehovah! We shudder to think of the implications for prayer of such an idea.

Evidence can also be drawn from the fact that the Bible describes God as the self-existent One, the eternal "I AM," and the "living God" who has "life in Himself." To be self-existent, God must be infinite in being and power or He would "run down" and "perish." God's existence must be infinite in order to be eternal, immutable, and perfect. Otherwise, we are left with a finite god no different from pagan deities who grow old and die.

> Great is our Lord, and abundant in strength,
> His understanding is infinite (Psalm 147:5).

In the context, God's glory is revealed by His omniscience because He can "count the number of the stars" and "give names to all of them" (v. 4). The universe may be vast and immeasurable to man but it is only a finite speck of dust to the Almighty. He knows its measurements because He made it.

In v. 5, the Psalmist gives a poetic contrast between the finite nature of the universe and the infinite nature of its Creator. He first says, "Great is our Lord." Leupold translates it as, "Great is our sovereign Lord," to catch the force of the Hebrew plural, a sort of plural of majesty.[1]

The Creator is the sovereign Lord of the universe. As such He is "abundant in strength," i.e., omnipotent. Since God is infinite in power, the creation of the world did not "drain" God. He was not "exhausted," "worn out," or "nearly out of gas" after speaking the worlds into being. But He is more than "abundant in power." But if we say that His power is finite, then there is a point at which it can be depleted or used up.

Now the Psalmist turns once again to the omniscience of God. He states that God's "understanding" or "knowledge" is "infinite." The Hebrew word translated "infinite" is a word that means without number, limitation, boundary, or end, i.e., infinite.

The Psalmist is using a poetic play on words by using the same word translated as "number" in verse 4, where God is said to be able "to count the number of the stars." He is able to do this because the stars are "limited," i.e., finite. They can be "numbered" because there is an "end" to them. There is a boundary to their number. We can draw a line and say that there are no more stars after this line.

But in contrast to the finite nature of the stars, it is impossible to "number" God's knowledge or understanding. It has no end, no boundaries, and no limitations. We cannot draw a line and say that God's knowledge ends with this line. The Hebrew word is emphatic, says Delitzsch:

> To His understanding there is no number, i.e. in its depth and fulness it cannot be defined by any number. What a comfort for the church as it traverses its ways, that are often so labyrinthine and entangled! Its Lord is the Omniscient as well as the Almighty One. Its history, like the universe, is a work of God's infinitely profound and rich understanding. It is a mirror of gracious love and righteous anger.[2]

The vision of God in Psalm 147 is an exalted one. The Lord is "great" because, as Moll points out:

> He has assigned a number to the stars which men cannot count (Gen. XV.5). This means that, in creating them, He called forth a number determined by Himself. It is also said that He calls all by name, i.e., that He knows and names them according to their special features, and employs them in His service according to His will, in conformity with the names which correspond to such a knowledge.

> The Omniscience and Omnipresence of God are thus presented at once to the soul. The greatness of God (v. 5) with respect to might (Job XXXVII.23) corresponds to the fullness of His understanding (Psa. CXLV.3), which no number can express. The same Lord who, with infinite power and unsearchable wisdom, rules the stars in their courses, rules also the world of man.[3]

The same vision of the infinite nature of God is found in Isaiah 40:12-17 where the entire universe is a like a "speck of dust" to the Almighty. The contrast between the finite nature of creation and the infinite nature of God is obvious.

Also, while the pagan gods were finite and could be "housed" in a temple because they were "contained" in the world, the Biblical God cannot not be "housed" or "contained" because He is infinite. If the earth is no more to Him than a "footstool," how can the world "contain" God? If the world cannot contain God, how much less could a temple "house" Him! (Isaiah 66:1-2; Matthew 5:35; Acts 7:49; 17:24-29).

Conclusion

Why do pagan philosophers such as Whitehead hate the infinite nature of God so much? God can be "infinite" only as long as He exists prior to, independent of, and apart from the world He made out of nothing. Thus the infinitude of God rests on the self-existence of God, the doctrine of Creation, and the timelessness of God.

But once God is *merged* into the world, or becomes identified as being the whole of it, or a part of it, He can no longer be infinite because He is no longer self-existent, the Creator, or timeless. Thus Whitehead's dipolar deity, finite gods such as Isis, or even a pantheistic god who is identified with the world, *cannot* be "infinite" by definition.

Neither can such a god create the world out of nothing. And, since the world "contains" god, then the world must be as "eternal" as he is. Since the world is eternal, and the world is "in" time, then time is eternal. Then nothing, not even god, is "timeless," for time is the ultimate and eternal "ground of being" for everything. Thus the hidden assumption of monism always lies behind every rejection of the timeless nature of the infinite/personal God of the Bible.

Questions for Discussion

1. What do we mean when we say that God is personal?
2. Is God infinite and personal at the same time?
3. What do we mean by "infinite?"
4. A God not quite inifinite or not quite personal would be a useless GOD. Why is this true?

ELEVEN

THE PERFECTION
OF GOD

The early Christians faced a world that was hostile to their idea that God is totally and absolutely "perfect." This was in conflict with the gods of the heathen who were *imperfect* because they were in the *process* of "growing" and "learning."

These gods were in the "process of becoming" because they were born, grew into maturity, and then eventually passed away into obscurity. They could "increase" and "decrease" in being, power, and knowledge. A god could go from strength to weakness just as easily as he could from weakness to strength.

Thus the gods of the pagans were not "perfect" because they were not "finished" or "complete." What they were today was not what they would be tomorrow. Their future was "open" because they could become good or evil, smaller or bigger, greater or lesser, ignorant or knowledgeable.

This "open" view of God tried to invade the early Church but it was condemned by the Church as a damnable heresy incompatible with Biblical Christianity. The idea that God was imperfect and still in the process of becoming something no one knew, not even God, was taught by Gnosticism, Valentinianism, Marcionism, and, later, by Socinianism. Today the same heresy is taught by processianism and moral government which have their roots in Whitehead's Platonic philosophy.

One of the chief reasons why the pagans gave up their gods and accepted the Christian God was that He was perfect while their gods were imperfect. God's perfection is part of the essence of His Godhood. This made Him not only *different* from the gods of the heathen but also *su-*

perior to them.

When Christian theology states that God is "perfect" it means that God is complete; finished; whole; lacking in nothing; not defective; has no blemishes or imperfections; does not increase or decrease; does not get smaller or bigger; does not grow older or younger; is not evolving; is not in the "process of becoming;" is not dependent but independent; and is the same eternal I AM who was, is, and forever shall be perfect in His existence, being, attributes, and works.

God's perfection is not an independent attribute. Perfection is a word that is essential to the definition of all the other attributes of God and raises them to divinity.

First, God is perfect in His existence in that He is the eternal self-existent One. His existence is "perfect" because it is complete, finished, whole, independent, not lacking in anything, needing nothing, does not increase or decrease, does not get older or younger, bigger or smaller, and is not evolving or "becoming." God's existence is thus not "open" but closed. It is not insecure but eternally secure.

Second, in the same exact way, God is perfect in His Being because He is complete, lacking nothing, and has no imperfections or blemishes that need correcting, does not need growth or development, will not get bigger or smaller, older or younger, and is not in need of any more "being" or "becoming."

Third, all of God's attributes are "perfect" and could not be divine attributes if they were not so. God is not partial but whole, not incomplete but finished, not defective but perfect.

Fourth, all of God's works are perfect because He is perfect. When He made the world, it could not have been anything but perfect and good. To deny that God is perfect means that we do not even have a perfect Bible, for an imperfect God can only give an imperfect revelation.

This is the root reason why the inerrancy of Scripture is denied by so many "evangelical" processians like Clark Pinnock. Once god is no longer viewed as perfect, how can he give a perfect revelation? Once you deny the Christian view of God, it will not be long before you deny the Christian view of the Bible, salvation, and eternal punishment.

God's Perfection and the Gospel

But does this issue mean anything to the average Christian? Yes, for the issue of the perfection of God either makes or breaks the Gospel itself. For example, is God's grace perfect or is there something wrong with it? Is it defective in some sense? Does it have blemishes? Is it in need of growth? If so, then it cannot serve as the basis of our salvation.

Likewise, is God's knowledge perfect? Or, is it imperfect, blemished, and lacking something? Does His knowledge get bigger or smaller, older or younger? Can it increase or decrease? Is God dependent on something or someone else to inform Him? Is His knowledge finite and incomplete, lacking many things? If so, then we cannot trust Him for He is as ignorant as we are.

Again, is God's power perfect or defective? Is it lacking in something? Does the Almighty need help? Is He in danger of running out of power? Does His power increase or decrease? If God's power is not perfect, then we cannot trust His power to keep us safe until He brings us to heaven. He may be too weak one day to defeat Satan.

Is God's goodness perfect? Is it complete, with no possibility of change? Or, is His goodness "open" to becoming evil? Must we wait every day for the "roll of the dice" to see if God is good? Or, is His goodness perfect?

When someone denies the perfection of God, he must be prepared to accept the consequences. The consistent processians are willing to do this. This is why they state that God can sin. They argue that God can lie and do evil and tempt others to do evil. This is what is meant by the "open view" of God! God is "open" to do evil but "closed" to sovereign acts of mercy and grace!

Some people have foolishly thought that they could deny the perfection of God's knowledge in order to get rid of the Biblical antinomy of divine sovereignty and human accountability without having to deny the perfection of all of God's attributes. What they fail to understand is that once imperfection, which is no more than the Greek philosophic concept of relativity, is injected into God, be it His knowledge or power, it destroys all of God.

For example, if God is not perfect in His knowledge, then He does not even have a perfect knowledge of Himself! He is unknown to Himself. He must wait until tomorrow for "the roll of the dice" to see what He will be. He doesn't even know if He will be a devil or an angel tomorrow!

It also means that He does not have a perfect knowledge of what man needs for salvation. He does not have a perfect knowledge of the present anymore than He has of the future. If God is not *perfect* in His goodness and in all His attributes, He is not a GOD worthy of our trust, love, or obedience. He is no different and in no way superior to the pagan gods.

No wonder the Scriptures and the Christian Church have always confessed that God is perfect in all His attributes and works. This is what made the Biblical God worthy to be GOD.

Biblical Passages

The word *perfect*, according to James means, "complete, lacking in nothing" (James 1:4). This word is directly applied to God in both the Old and the New Testaments.

> Ascribe greatness to our God!
> The Rock! His work is perfect (Deuteronomy 32:3-4).

Our God is "great," says Moses, because He is "perfect" in all His works. The Hebrew word *tamim* means that which is complete, lacking nothing, whole, pure, with no defects or imperfections whatsoever. The word was used in its physical sense to describe the lamb used for Passover. This lamb had to be "perfect," i.e., without any defects, imperfections, or blemishes. The lamb could be lacking in nothing. It had to be complete (Exodus 12:5). In the same way, whatever God does is "perfect."

> As for God, His way is blameless; . . .
> For who is God, besides the Lord?
> And who is a rock, besides our God (2 Samuel 22:31-32)?

The marginal notes of the NASV correctly point out that the word translated "blameless" literally means "complete." It is once again the word *tamim* and is translated as "perfect" in the KJV.

The word *blameless* opens up another aspect of the doctrine of the perfection of God. If God is not perfect in His attributes, then we must conclude that He is not *morally* perfect! This at once "opens" God to moral guilt or blame. The Bible views "perfection" in the moral sense as "blamelessness." The "open" view of God leaves Him "open" to make mistakes caused by His ignorance and weakness! But if God is perfect in all He does, then He is blameless in all He does.

> Stand and consider the wonders of God. . . .
> The wonders of One perfect in knowledge (Job 37:14, 16).

Delitzsch translates verse 16 as,

> The wondrous things of Him
>> who is perfect in knowledge.

He comments that,

> God is called . . . the Omniscient One, whose knowledge is absolute
> as to its depths as well as its circumference.[1]

God is not lacking in knowledge in any sense. He is not defective or imperfect in His knowledge of the past, present, or future of the world He made. "The Law of the Lord is perfect" (Psalm 19:7).

The Bible is the inerrant Word of God because it is as perfect as the God who inspired it. Only a perfect God can give a perfect revelation.

> Neither is He served by human hands, as though He needed anything,
> since He Himself gives to all life and breath and all things (Acts 17:25).

In order to show the difference between his God and the gods of the Greek philosophers, the Apostle Paul declares that his God is "not in need of anything," i.e., perfect. He is the self-existent One who lacks in nothing. "The will of God is . . . perfect" (Romans 12:2).

Not only are God's ways, words, works, wisdom, and knowledge perfect but also His will. In that it is "perfect," it is also "good," "acceptable," and "blameless."

Conclusion

The fact that God's Word plainly states that God's knowledge is perfect is enough to prove that the Almighty is cognizant of all things including the future. But rationalists will not believe it unless they know "how," "in what way," and "why" God is perfect when man is not. They reject the plain teaching of Scripture and follow their own conceited ideas of what God is like.

While we may not be able to answer all the riddles that the pagans compose, we do know that we cannot run through the attributes of God selecting what we like and throwing out the rest. The attributes of God are not independent of each other but are so interrelated that if one is removed, they all fall. Either we accept all of God as He has revealed Himself, or we are left with nothing at all.

Questions for Discussion

1. Were the gods of the heathens perfect?
2. What made the biblical God stand out?
3. What do we mean when we say that God is "perfect?"
4. If someone says that God is not perfect, is his God GOD or only a man-made god?
5. Does the Bible describe God as perfect?

TWELVE

THE ETERNITY OF GOD

C hristian theology has always begun its discussion of the relationship of God to time and eternity with the doctrine of Creation because this is where the Bible begins (Genesis 1:1). In the first verse of the Bible we are told that God *alone* is eternal. Everything else, be it invisible or visible, spiritual or material, is *not* eternal because God created *all* things. Thus God alone existed *before* all things and all things depend on His power for their existence.

This is also clearly taught in the New Testament.

> For by Him all things were created, both in the heavens and on earth, visible and invisible, whether thrones or dominions or rulers or authorities — all things have been created through Him and for Him. And He is before all things, and in Him all things hold together (Colossians 1:16-17).

In this passage, the Apostle Paul was emphatic that *nothing* existed alongside of God for all eternity. All things are created and hence not eternal. In order to make this clear he encompasses everything in heaven and in earth regardless of its spiritual or material nature. Whatever we may ask about has been created by God.

It is for this reason that Christians have always taught that space and time were both created and hence are not eternal. While the Greeks believed that space and time were eternal, and even deified time and made it into the god Kronos, the Christians rejected such an idea because space and time are attributes of *created* things.

Created things, by definition, occupy space and time. They are limited because they can only be in *one* place at any *one* time. Space and time are inseparable, like the two sides of a coin.

But is this true of the God of the Bible? Can He be in *more* places at one time or is He limited like Zeus and Baal? Are space and time eternal? Is God limited by them? Does He exist in them? Or, do they exist in Him?

The Vocabulary of Eternity

Every Hebrew and Greek word that could possibly signify "eternity" was applied to God in the Bible. Since He alone is the "eternal" God, the word *eternal* became one of the names of God, signifying one of the essential attributes that makes Him GOD as opposed to the pagan gods (Genesis 21:33; Romans 16:26).

The eternity of God is the basis of our confidence in His ability to care for us. Thus Moses could speak of "the everlasting arms of God" as carrying and protecting us because He is "the eternal God" (Deuteronomy 33:27).

The Hebrews used the word *olam* (forever, everlasting, eternal) in creative constructs in order to emphasize that God *alone* was the "Eternal I AM." God is viewed as being from "eternity" to "eternity" in such places as Psalm 41:13; 90:2; 106:48. If God were "in" time like the pagan deities, then He would have a "beginning" and an "end." But God has no beginning or end because He is from "eternity" to "eternity."

Even as Isaiah said,

> . . . thus saith the high and lofty One that *inhabiteth eternity*, whose name is Holy; I dwell in the high and lofty place (Isaiah 57:15 KJV, emphasis added).

While the NASV's text says, "lives forever," its margin records the literal Hebrew as "dwell in eternity." Other modern versions emphasize that God here claims that He alone has existed or lived from all eternity.

> Even from eternity I am He; and there is none who can deliver out of my hand; I act and who can reverse? (Isaiah 43:13)

The Hebrew simply says that God was the I AM "before the day." This is interpreted in the Greek Septuagint and the Latin Vulgate in the sense of "before the first day," i.e., before time itself began." The ancient and classical commentators all see God as claiming that He pre-existed time itself and is "eternal" in this sense.

Eternity and the Other Attributes

We have discussed the issue of the timelessness of God in connection with the other attributes of God to emphasize that timelessness cannot be separated from the Christian view of God. Everything that the Bible tells us about God is said in the context of His timelessness. All His attributes are *timeless* attributes.

God's existence is described as "eternal" because it is self-existent and independent. As such, it is perfect and does not increase or decrease. He always was, is, and shall be the same eternal I AM. He alone is eternal because He alone is GOD.

God's being and attributes are also described as "eternal" because they are likewise independent and self-existent. Thus Paul could speak of "His eternal power and divine nature" (Romans 1:20).

Since God's knowledge is part of the "divine nature," it too is eternal, independent, self-existent, and perfect. Therefore, any attempt to say that God's knowledge "grows" is a denial that it is eternal. The only way it can "grow" is for it to be dependent on time and space. Thus it is not self-existent. If it is not eternal, self-existent, independent, or perfect, wherein is it "divine"? It is more *human* than divine!

Is Time God?

The only way to deny that God is eternal in the sense of "timeless" is to hold that time is *not* created but is itself eternal. But for time to be eternal means that it must be self-existent and not dependent on anything, not even God. Like Zoroastrian dualism, in which two gods struggle to overcome each other, time becomes a rival "god" to Jehovah.

One of the more consistent modern pagan thinkers has been forced to the same conclusions. Stephen Davis argues that God is not timeless because such an idea is not "coherent" to him.

> . . . a timeless being cannot be the Christian God . . . [because] the notion of a timeless being is probably incoherent.[1]

As a rationalist, Davis demands complete coherence.

> If we want to be rational we have no choice but to reject what we judge
> to be incoherent.[2]

In the place of the historic Christian doctrine that God is timeless,
Davis proposes to "argue for the assumption that God is temporally
eternal."[3] But if God is only "temporally eternal" and not timeless, this
means that time is itself eternal and not created. And if it is eternal, then
it does not depend on God for its existence.

> Time is not a contingent, created thing like the universe.[4]

Since time was not created, then it must eternally exist alongside of
God. Davis states that, "time has always existed alongside God."[5] But
for time to exist alongside of God means that it too must be "divine"
in that it is self-existent and not dependent on anything outside of itself
including God. Time is not created.

> . . . time was not created; it necessarily exists . . it depends for its ex-
> istence on nothing else.[6]

But which is "higher," God or time? Which is the "ground of existence" for the other? Is time "in" God or is God "in" time? Which of
these two eternal gods is the "greater"? Davis decides that time is. Davis
ends up believing in, "a temporal God who is 'in' time."[7]

The process is finally complete. Instead of being the creature, Time
is now the "Creator" of everything including God! Jehovah has been
kicked off His throne and Kronos put in His place! We have returned
full circle back to the Greek view that TIME is GOD!

The Christian view has always taught that time was created by and
dependent on the one true God who alone is self-existent and eternal.
Thus time is "in" God as He is its Creator and Lord. But with Davis
and other processians, time is not created but eternal, self-existent, and
independent of God. Time not only eternally existed outside of and alongside of God, but time is a higher god "in" whom God must find the
ground of His own existence!

When we look to Davis, Pinnock, or Olson to give just one Biblical
text saying that time is not created; that it is eternal; that it has always
existed outside of and alongside of God; that it is self-existent and in-

dependent of God; that God is dependent upon it; that God is "in" time; we look in vain. No one has ever come forth with such a text.

The entire argument against the timeless nature of God is merely *philosophical* and devoid of any Biblical support. After all, Genesis 1:1 does *not* say, "In the beginning Time." But it *does* say, "In the beginning God." The world was not created by Time *and* God. God alone is the Creator of *all* things including time.

When we took a close look at the philosophical arguments against the timelessness of God, we came to the conclusion that they were highly overrated and patently absurd. If the same line of reasoning is applied to space as well as time, the absurdity of the argument is obvious. If the arguments that are used to deny the omniscience of God are valid, then they would also refute His omnipresence. While the Socinians and Jehovah's Witnesses have already taken this next logical step, most "evangelical" processians are either not intellectually honest enough to admit it or emotionally ready for it.

- To say that God cannot act in time without being limited by time is the same as saying that He cannot act in space without being limited by it.

- To say that if God is timeless then time is an illusion is the same as saying that if God is spaceless then space is an illusion.

- To say that if God is timeless He cannot know the categories of time is the same as saying that if God is spaceless, He cannot know the categories of space.

- To say that since the Bible uses metaphors of time such as "past," "present," and "future" and such words as "foreknowledge," that God is limited by time is the same as saying that because the Bible uses metaphors of space such as "up," "down," "here," and "there" as in "God came down," that He is limited by space.

- To say that God cannot hear our prayers unless He is limited by time is to say that He cannot hear our prayers unless He is limited by space.

- To say that unless God is "in" time like man, man has a greater knowledge than God, is to say that unless He is "in" space like man, man has a greater knowledge than God.

The philosophical arguments against the doctrine of the timelessness of God are stupid as well as blasphemous. This is how the Fathers and the Reformers viewed such heretical attacks on the Divine Glory of God.

Conclusion

God is the Maker of all things including time. Nothing is "above" or "beneath" God as if He needed something to support Him. No eternal rivals are alongside God because He alone is the eternal infinite/personal God who is the sovereign Creator and Sustainer of all things. To Him be all the glory!

Questions for Discussion

1. Is God alone eternal or is something else as eternal as God?
2. What did the Apostle Paul say in Col. 1:16-17?
3. What has always been the teaching of the Christian Church?
4. Some people claim that Time is eternal. Does this make Time into another God?
5. Does the Bible ever describe time or space as eternal?

THIRTEEN

THE IMMUTABILITY OF GOD

The historic Christian doctrine of the immutability of God is under special attack these days. The processians are particularly vicious in vilifying this doctrine by misrepresenting it.

Clark Pinnock is a good example of this procedure. He begins by calling God's immutability "Platonic" thinking based on a "Greek model."[1] He then argues that if God is immutable, "there cannot be genuine freedom."[2] He even claims that it came from "Aristotle's God."[3]

According to Pinnock, the orthodox view teaches that that God is "static" and "immovable." Then, having defined the doctrine by using Greek concepts, he turns around and condemns it as Greek philosophy! This is the logical fallacy known as "stacking the deck" or "building a straw man."

The early Church did not accept "thought thinking itself," the god of Aristotle. They condemned Aristotle as an atheist because he did not believe in a God who existed prior to, independent of, and apart from the world which He made out of nothing. Also, Aristotle believed in many finite gods. Thus he was an idolater as well as an atheist.

Christian theology derived its doctrine of the immutability of God from the Holy Scriptures and not from the atheistic philosophers of the ancient world. The God who has revealed Himself in Scripture is "faithful," "dependable," and "unchanging." This is what historic Christianity has confessed for two thousand years.

The processians consistantly misrepresent the Christian doctrine of the immutability of God because, as humanists, they begin with false assumptions.

First, they assume the Greek dichotomy that God must be either Parmenides' static "being" or Heraclitus' dynamic "becoming." Humanistic theology will only recognize two gods. This is why they constantly harp on the "static versus dynamic" theme.

The history of philosophy demonstrates that humanistic views of God swing back and forth between a static god and a dynamic god. In one century they will champion a "static" god, and then in the next century they will champion a "dynamic" god. They simply "rebel" against the previous generation's god.

The contrast between the "static" god found in eighteenth-century Rationalism with the "dynamic" liberal god of the nineteenth century is a perfect example of how humanistic thought swings back and forth between Parmenides' god and Heraclitus' god.

It is also interesting to point out that when Parmenides's static god was in vogue among rationalists, the Christian God was rejected because He was too "dynamic." Today, now that Heraclitus' dynamic god is in vogue, the rationalists reject the Christian God because He is too "static"! Either way the God of the Bible loses out.

Second, the processians assume that when Christians speak of the "immutability" of God, they mean an "immobility" of God in which He does nothing and knows nothing. Why is this?

Some of the philosophic gods of the heathen are said to be "immutable" in the sense of "immobile," "unmoving," "unacting," "uncaring," and "unknowing," because they are nonpersonal gods that are defined as "ground of being," "power," or "energy."

We agree that a nonpersonal "it" cannot hear our prayers or interact with us. But we emphatically disagree with the attempt to impute such pagan concepts to the Christian doctrine of the immutability of God. It would help their case if the processians could produce just one orthodox theologian who denies the personhood of God. But they have never submitted such evidence.

The Christian View of God's Immutability

The Christian doctrine of God does not operate on the assumption that either Parmenides or Heraclitus had the "true" view of God. Such atheistical philosophers are best ignored as just another example of the "foolishness of the world." Our view of God must come from revelation alone.

The Christian God is in stark contrast to the gods of the heathen, who were *mutable* and hence always changing. The gods were born, grew old, and could even die. They could change morally and become good or evil. They could even change sexes, with male gods becoming female deities and vice versa. The Marcionite heretics even claimed that the god of the Old Testament was different from the god of the New Testament!

In the Christian view, God is immutable, changeless, consistent, faithful, dependable, the same yesterday, today, and forever in His existence, being, and attributes.

What does all this mean? It means that when we pray, we pray to the *same* God twice. The God who created the world is the *same* God who later spoke to Abraham, Isaac, and Jacob, who gave His law to Moses, sent His Son to be our Savior, inspired Paul, and in whom we believe today. He is the *exact* same God and not something *different*. The God of the New Testament is not *different* from the God of the Old Testament. He is not older, wiser, more knowledgeable, bigger or smaller, greater or lesser, stronger or weaker. Only ONE God, as the eternal I AM, is the same yesterday, today, and forever.

Notice that we did not say in our definition that God was immutable in His "works." The Scriptures do not teach that God is immutable in terms of His *relationship* to His creation. He is not "sitting on His hands doing nothing." He is the sovereign Creator and Sustainer of all things.

The Lord Jehovah invades and pervades both space and time and does His mighty deeds. His glory is revealed in every flash of lightning and peal of thunder. The roar of the sea is a testimony of His power. His providential care can be seen in His concern for the smallest sparrow. He makes the grass to grow and sends the rain. The mighty lions look to God for their food. The Lord God Omnipotent reigns over His creation (see Psalm 22; 104; 148).

By His omnipotent power, God intervenes in the affairs of men, raising up and putting down, killing and bringing to life. He interacts with men and changes His revelation, laws, and deeds from covenant to covenant. He is so involved by His providence in the affairs of the sons of men that His hand lies behind all things. Nations even rise and fall at His command (see 1 Samuel 2:6-10).

Those who are the "sons of Satan" are under Divine wrath. But God can change His attitude toward us, and we can become the "sons of God" under His blessing. Salvation is a transition from wrath to grace in which God's attitude toward us changes (Ephesians 2:1-4).

How different is this doctrine from the gods of the heathen who, if personal, are *subject* to change all the time or, if nonpersonal, know no change at all!

Both Static and Dynamic

God is thus not trapped into being either static or dynamic. He is both and neither. While in His relationship to the world He is the dynamic sovereign Lord of history, in His existence, being, and attributes, He is changeless.

First, God is not capable of change in terms of His existence. He cannot go out of existence like a flickering candle. He will not grow old or die. The eternal I AM will always be the same.

Second, God is immutable in His being and nature. He cannot become "non-God." He cannot become less or more than what He has always been. There are no "degrees" of God, as if He were sliding up and down some pagan scale of being. God is GOD and always was GOD and always shall be GOD. We do not have to wait for God to become GOD, contrary to what processians like Whitehead, Davis, Rice, and Pinnock claim.

This is why Christian theology has always been careful to say that Christ is *both* GOD and man. But if God is not perfect or immutable and is still awaiting the time when He shall become GOD, then Christ could not be GOD!

The divine nature of Christ as well as the divine inspiration of Scripture become absolutely impossible once the perfection and immutability of God are rejected. This is the conclusion that most modern processians have now accepted.

As a matter of historical record, we must add that *all* essential Christian doctrines from the Trinity to the atonement were conceived and confessed with the assumption that God is the infinite/personal, eternal, perfect, immutable, omniscient, omnipotent, omnipresent, transcendent, sovereign, immutable Creator of Heaven and earth.

This was the theology behind *all* the ancient creeds of the Church from the Apostles' Creed and the Nicene Creed to the Athanasian Creed, and *all* the creeds of the Reformation from the Augsburg Confession and the Thirty-nine Articles to the Westminster Confession of Faith. Thus it does not surprise us in the least that modern theology is slowly but surely rejecting *everything* these creeds confess. Once the Christian God is rejected, it is only a matter of time before all Christian doctrine is rejected.

Can God Become Evil?

The Bible clearly describes the Creator as "changeless." Immutability in this sense is applied to all the attributes of God and this makes God different from and superior to the gods of the heathen. For example, when Christians say that God is good, they mean He always was, is, always shall be, and cannot be anything other than good. In other words, He is *immutably* good. Thus He *cannot* do evil because He cannot *become* evil. We can trust Him for His goodness is "unalterable," "eternally consistent," and "ever the same." The problem of evil is solved by the Biblical teaching that God *cannot* do evil.

In contrast, processians such as Stephen Davis argue that God *can* become evil because He *can* sin. But this "open view" of God is possible only if God is imperfect or immutable. If God is neither perfect nor immutable, then He can sin. Thus the historic Christian doctrine of the impeccability of God and Christ is also rejected by such thinkers.

But in trying to absolve God from the problem of evil by reducing Him down to the level of Zeus or Baal, modern rationalists have actually accomplished what they set out to avoid. The moment they denied the perfection and immutability of God, they unwittingly established that God *can* become the author of evil *tomorrow!*

The more daring and bold among the processians state God *can* become the Devil! This is what they *must* say if they are consistent. After all, if the universe is *really* based on pure chance or contingency, and God does not know or ordain the future, then *anything* is possible — including God's becoming Satan!

How different is the attitude of Christian theology, which has always taught that God is *immutably* good, i.e., He *cannot* be the author of evil because He cannot become evil, do evil, or tempt anyone to do evil.

Biblical Passages

"Shall not the Judge of all the earth deal justly" (Genesis 18:25)? To Abraham, God was *immutably* just. It was inconceivable to him that God could do anything that was unjust because God is a righteous God and all His acts must be consistent with His nature. Thus God would do the right thing when it came time to deal with Sodom and Gomorrah.

We must also point out that such passages as this reveal that God does not have the absolute "freedom" found in Greek philosophy. The Greeks assumed that the gods were "free" to become demons if they so chose. Nothing was impossible to them.

But the Biblical God is "free" to act only in conformity to His nature. Thus God "*cannot* lie" because "it is *impossible*" (Titus 1:2; Hebrews 6:18, emphasis added). God is not free to become non-God or to do non-Godlike things. While He is free to do righteousness and to speak the truth, He is not "free" to do evil or speak lies, because He is not capable of doing so.

In the same way, man can act only in conformity to his nature. He cannot do that which is inconsistent with his nature. Thus the humanistic vision of a truly autonomous man who can do anything and everything in a world of chance is a delusion because the Greek ideal of absolute freedom is an illusion.

> And God said to Moses, "I AM WHO I AM"; and He said, "Thus you shall say to the sons of Israel, I AM has sent me to you (Exodus 3:14).

Even such names of God as "I AM" bear witness to the immutability of God. God is ever the same God. He is the eternal *I AM* because His nature is complete. He did not say, "I BECOME," but "I AM."

> God is not a man, that He should lie, nor a son of man, that He should repent. Has He said, and will He not do it? Or has He spoken, and will He not make it good (Numbers 23:19)?

> And also the Glory of Israel will not lie or change His mind; for He is not a man that He should change His mind (1 Samuel 15:29).

These texts clearly state that those who say that God can lie, that God can do evil, that God can repent, that God can promise to do something and then fail to do it, have made a god in the image of man. But God is *not* like mutable man, who is capable of lying because of his sinful and mutable nature. Neither is God like man, who needs to repent for doing evil.

According to Scripture, God is immutably faithful and true. Thus He is not "open" to lying or to failing to make good on His promises. Indeed, without the basis of the immutability of God, all the promises of God are rendered null and void. After all, a mutable God who is "open" to failure and sin cannot give man immutable promises to live and die by!

If we live in a universe where all things including God are "open," i.e., governed by chance, then we must wait for the "roll of the dice" to see if God's promises come true. God's promises are thus reduced to mere wishes and guesses which may or may not be fulfilled because not even God knows the future.

But if God is *immutably* and *perfectly* faithful and true, then we *know* that He will do all He has promised. His promises are not made in ignorance as some kind of "shot in the dark." He promises what He *knows* will happen because He guarantees it to come to pass by His almighty power.

> The Rock! His work is perfect,
> For all His ways are just;
> A God of faithfulness and without injustice,
> Righteous and upright is He (Deuteronomy 32:3-4).

One of the metaphors used in Scripture to illustrate the immutability of God is "The Rock." (See Genesis 49:24; Deuteronoy 32:15, 18, 30, 31; 1 Samuel 2:2; 2 Samuel 22:2, 3, 32, 47; 3:3; Psalm 18:2, 31, 46; 28:1; 31:2, 3; 42:9; 61:2; 62:2, 6, 7; 71:3; 78:35; 89:26; 92:15; 94:22; 1 Corinthians 10:4.) In the passage quoted, Keil and Delitzsch point out that the word *Rock*

> . . . is placed first absolutely, to give it the greater prominence. God is called "the Rock," as the unchangeable refuge, who grants a firm defense and secure resort to His people, by virtue of His unchangeableness or impregnable firmness . . . David, who had so often experienced the rock-like protection of his God, adopted it in his Psalms.[4]

Notice also that God's greatness, perfection, justice, faithfulness, purity, righteousness, and uprightness all flow out of and thus are intrinsically bound together with His immutable rocklike nature. God is called the "Rock" in Scripture in order to distinguish Him from mutable man. This is in stark contrast to the god of the processians, which can only be described as some kind of divine "Putty" that time and space mold.

The fact that God's perfection and immutability are joined together in this text from the Mosaic period also supplies us with an iron-clad refutation of the claim that the idea that God is perfect and immutable comes from Greek philosophy. Modern processians such as Pinnock dismiss the historic Christian doctrine of God by the cheap rebuff that it "is simply the Greek ideal of perfection."[5]

Of course, processians like Pinnock nowhere *document* the Greek origins of the Christian God. And, indeed, it will take a great deal of imagination to picture Moses and the prophets learning about God from Greek philosophers who were not even born until hundreds of years later!

The fact that the Bible, beginning in Genesis, speaks of the infinite/personal God who is the Creator and Ruler of all things forever reveals the Greek-origin charge as just another cheap Socinian trick.

> Thy years are throughout all generations.
> Of old Thou didst found the earth;
> And the heavens are the work of Thy hands.
> Even they will perish, but Thou dost endure;
> And all of them will wear out like a garment;
> Like clothing Thou wilt change them,
>   and they will be changed.
> But Thou are the same,
> And Thy years will not come to an end (Psalm 102:24-27).

The eternity and immutability of God are revealed and celebrated in this Psalm. That it is also applied to Jesus in Hebrews 1:1-12 makes it even more glorious.

The Psalmist begins by contrasting the shortness of human life with the eternity of God in verses 23-24. He then turns to consider the world around him. Instead of ascribing eternity to it as do the pagans, the Psalmist proclaims that it was created by the true God who existed prior to it, independent of it, and apart from it.

The world is dependent on its Creator for its very existence. It cannot exist autonomously apart from God. Indeed, He made the world with a mutable or changeable nature in that it decays and perishes. Just as a piece of cloth gets thinner and thinner until it must be thrown away, the world will one day perish. Then God will create a new heavens and a new earth.

While the world is mutable, decaying, and will perish one day, Jehovah is not like this at all. He is the eternal I AM, the Unchanging One. He is not "changing," "decaying," or "perishing." He is ever the same. But He could not be the *same* from eternity to eternity if He were changing into something new and different all the time. He can only be "the same" if He is what He has always been and what He will always be.

Down through the centuries, this passage has always been central in the Christian concept of God. The world may change but God does not change. Thus He is our refuge and our strength. Notice the profound comments of the great expositors of these verses.

Charles Spurgeon

When heaven and earth shall flee away from the dread presence of the great Judge, he will be unaltered by the terrible confusion, and the world in conflagration will effect no change in him; even so, the Psalmist remembered that when Israel was vanquished, her capital destroyed, and her temple levelled with the ground, her God remained the same self-existent, all-sufficient being, and would restore his people, even as he will restore the heavens and the earth, bestowing at the same time a new glory never known before. The doctrine of the immutability of God should be more considered than it is, for the neglect of it tinges the theology of many religious teachers, and makes them utter many things of which they would have seen the absurdity long ago if they had remembered the divine declaration, "I am God, I change not, therefore ye sons of Jacob are not consumed."[6]

Stephen Charnock

The text doth not only assert the eternal duration of God, but his immutability in that duration; his eternity is signified in that expression, "thou shalt endure;" his immutability in this, "thou are the same. . . . " He could not be the same if he could be changed into any other thing than what he is. The psalmist therefore puts, not thou *hast been* or *shall be*, but *thou art* the same, without any alteration. . . . The psalmist here alludes to the name *Jehovah, I am*, and doth ascribe immutability to God, but exclude everything else from partaking in that perfection.[7]

Lange's Commentary

Although the heavens and the mountains are termed everlasting with reference to the lasting duration of the order of things, . . . yet, when contrasted with God, they are not merely transitory and mutable, but will undergo a change by the power of God. In view of the contrast to this change to which the world will be subjected, [verse 28] is not to be understood as referring . . . to the fact that God is the only Being who can lay claim to the Divine name, but, as in Job iii.19; Isa. xli.4; xlvi.4, to the immutability in which God ever manifests himself as the *same*.[8]

J. A. Alexander

The meaning then is, Thou art the Unchangeable One just described.[9]

Franz Delitzsch

The expressive [Hebrew phrase], Thou art He, *i.e.*, unalterably the same One, is also taken from the mouth of the prophet, Isa. xli.4, xliii.10, xlvi.4, xlviii.12; [the word "same"] is a predicate, and denotes the identity (sameness) of Jahve.[10]

Matthew Henry

It is likewise comfortable in reference to the decay and death of our own bodies, and the removal of our friends from us, that God is an everlasting God, and that therefore, if he be ours, in him we may have everlasting consolation. In this plea observe how, to illustrate the eternity of the Creator, he compares it with the mutability of the creature; for it is God's sole prerogative to be unchangeable. . . . God is perpetual and everlasting: Thou art the same, subject to no change.[11]

Jehovah is the one true God, for He is eternal and immutable. In Him we can trust, for He is ever the same and changeth not.

For I, the LORD, do not change (Malachi 3:6).

For the Christian, this passage alone is sufficient to confirm that the historic faith of the Christian Church in the immutability of God arises out of Scripture. In the context, God claims that because He is unchanging, unalterable, and immutable, He does not destroy His people Israel. He will keep His covenant with Abraham and thus "the sons of Jacob are not consumed" (Malachi 3:6). Let us again glance at some classic comments on this passage.

Matthew Henry

Here we have God's immutability asserted by himself, and gloried in. . . . We may all apply this very sensibly to ourselves; because we have to do with a God that *changes not*, therefore it is that *we are not consumed*. . . . [12]

E. B. Pusey

The proper name of God, He Who Is, involves His Unchangeableness. For change implies imperfection; it changes to that which is either more perfect or less perfect: to somewhat which that being, who changes, is not or has not. But God has everything in Himself perfectly.[13]

C. F. Keil

The unchangeableness of God is implied in the name *Jehovah*, "who is that He is," the absolutely independent and absolutely existing One.[14]

Thomas V. Moore

Let not the Christian heart grow timid in a time of prevalent wickedness and unbelief, in the fear that the ark of God may perish. The sons of Jacob shall not be consumed — the seed of Christ shall not perish. The unchangeableness of God is the sheet-anchor of the Church. He will be faithful to his Son, and to his word, however disheartening external circumstances may appear to our wavering faith.

The perseverance of the saints is guaranteed, not by their unchangeable love to God, but by his unchangeable love to them, and his eternal purpose and promise in Christ Jesus.[15]

These commentators point out that our reliance on God to do as He has promised is based on the immutability of His nature. But if God as well as all things are being tossed to and fro in some kind of Heraclitian flux, as the processians claim, then the god who promises something today will not be the same god tomorrow. He may have learned some new things and thus decided not to keep his word. Such a god is not trustworthy.

Jesus Christ is the same yesterday and today, yes and forever (Hebrews 13:8).

Having already ascribed Psalm 102:25-27 to Christ in Hebrews 1:10-12, the author of Hebrews concludes with a ringing affirmation of the immutability of Christ in 13:8. But can the second Person of the Trinity be the "same yesterday, today, and forever" if God is mutable? If Jesus is "open" in the sense of the processian's chance-based world, then we cannot pray to the same Jesus twice! As a matter of fact, the processian Jesus is *never* the same. He is always changing. But is this the Jesus of the Christian Gospel? We think not.

> Him who is and who was and who is to come (Revelation 1:4).

The syntax of the Greek text of Revelation 1:4 is absolutely clear that Christ is immutable for what He *is* right now, is what He always *was* and what He shall always *be*. It is the Greek equivalent of the Hebrew, "I Am that I Am."

This is also why God is called "the First and the Last" and "The Beginning and the End." He is the *same* from the beginning to the end of the world (Isaiah 41:4; 44:6; 48:12; Revelation 1:17; 2:8; 22:13).

> The Father of lights, with whom there is no variation, or shifting shadow (James 1:17).

In this passage, James speaks of God as the unchanging and unchangeable One, He who is ever the same from age to age.

The context of James's statement on the immutability of God is also important. In the context James is discussing the origin of sin. The fact that God cannot be blamed for evil is based on the immutably good nature of God. In verse 16, he warns Christians, "do not be deceived, my beloved brethren." The expression, "Do not be deceived" is always associated with subjects which heretics try to use to deceive the elect (see 1 Corinthians 15:33; Galatians 6:7). As we have already seen, heretics usually use "the problem of evil" in order to undermine the faith of Christians. Christians must be on their guard, says James, not to be misled by heretics on this subject.

James is quite aware that the pagan religions in his own day taught that god was the author of sin. It is this blasphemous idea that he attacks in this opening chapter of his book. He first states that God cannot be the author of sin because He is *incapable* of doing evil by nature. Thus He *cannot* be tempted by sin. Neither is He capable of tempting anyone into sin.

> Let no one say when he is tempted, "I am being tempted by God";
> for God cannot be tempted by evil, and He Himself does not tempt
> anyone (James 1:13).

Notice that James proceeds from God's nature to His actions. God "cannot" by nature be tempted by evil. He is not "open" to sin. Therefore He "does not" in His actions tempt anyone to do evil. Notice also that James does not say that God could do evil if He "wanted," but that God "cannot" even be tempted by it, much less do it. In other words, God is not "free" to do anything that is inconsistent with His nature.

But if God *cannot* be the "author" of evil, who is? James points his finger at *man*.

> But each one is tempted when he is carried away and enticed by his own lust. Then when lust has conceived, it gives birth to sin; and when sin is accomplished, it brings forth death (James 1:14-15).

But what about God? Does James go on to say that God was not the author of evil because He did not foresee it? If the processians are right in limiting the power and knowledge of God, isn't this an ideal place for such an idea to be given? It is nowhere to be found! James does not limit the knowledge and power of God, but rather exalts them as immutable.

James goes on to guarantee that God will never become the author of evil by contrasting God to the "lights" He has placed in the heavens. While the sun, moon, and stars wax and wane, i.e., change because they are mutable, there is "no variation" with God or a "shifting shadow."

After meticulously tracing the two Greek words translated as "no variation" and "shifting shadow" throughout ancient sacred and secular literature, Joseph Mayor concludes,

> The meaning of the passage will then be "God is alike incapable of change in his nature (*parallage*) and incapable of being changed by the action of others (*aposkiasma*).[16]

Notice that by using these two different words, James tells us that the immutability of God includes the idea that people, places, and events *cannot change God*. The idea that God is changing as events happen would be deemed blasphemous by James.

The Latin Vulgate renders the words as, *apud quem non est transmutatio nec, vicissitudinis obumbratio.* God is *not* "transmuting" into GOD. God *is* GOD and has always been so and will always be so throughout eternity.

The Repentance of God

But what about the few passages in Scripture that speak of God's "repenting?" (See Genesis 6:6; Exodus 32:14; 1 Samuel 15:11, 35.) Do these pose any problem to the doctrine of the immutability of God?

First, we have already stated that the immutability of God concerns the *being* of God. None of the passages in question speak of a change in God's *nature*, but rather describe some *act* of God. Second, all of these passages describe a change in God's works in terms of His revelation, relationship, or attitude toward man.

In Genesis 6:6, because of man's sin, God changed His attitude toward mankind from acceptance to rejection, from joy to grief, from tolerance to judgment.

In Ephesians 2:1-4, God's attitude changes toward us from wrath to grace when we come to accept His Son.

In Exodus 32:14, God changed the revelation of His will. He first told Moses that He was going to destroy Israel (v. 10). Then He revealed that He was not going to destroy Israel due to the intercession of Moses (v. 14).

The same thing can be said of the sacrifice of Isaac. God's revealed will first commanded Abraham to sacrifice his son (Genesis 22:2). Then as he lifted the knife, God revealed that he was not to kill his son (Genesis 22:12).

First Samuel 15 is a perfect example of the difference between God's being unchanging in His nature while being capable of change in His relationship to men. In verses 11 and 35, the Lord "repented," i.e., changed His revealed mind or will concerning Saul. Since Saul had rejected God's Word, God now rejected Saul's kingship, and David has to be anointed king in his place (v. 26).

But lest we assume that God can change in His nature, Samuel adds in verse 29 that God,

> . . . . will not lie nor repent: for he is not a man that he should repent (KJV).

Thus in the same chapter where we are told twice that God "repented," we are also told that God never repents! The liberal theologian will jump at this and cry "contradiction." But we doubt that the author of 1 Samuel 15 was really so stupid as to compose so blatant a contradiction. Instead, Samuel is reassuring us that the Lord is unchanging in His being and nature even when He changes the revelation of His will or His attitude toward man. The NASV and other modern versions simply translate that God "regretted" or "grieved" instead of "repented." In this way, it can be clearly seen that it is God's attitude which is spoken of and not His essence or nature.

God's revelation of laws, institutions, and ceremonies change from covenant to covenant. Thus we can go from circumcision to baptism, Passover to the Lord's Supper, from the ceremonial law to freedom in Christ. But none of this requires a change in the being or nature of God. Only His administration changes.

Conclusion

As one of the perfections of God, the immutability of God is found throughout the Scriptures. It is viewed as an essential aspect of the greatness and glory of God. It is the foundation of the believer's hope and trust. And it enables us to live with confidence knowing that the Triune God is "the same yesterday, today, and forever."

Questions for Discussion

1. What did Greek philosophy mean when it talked about "immutability?"
2. What do Christians mean by "immutability?"
3. Is God immutable according to the Bible?
4. If God is not immutable, do we have any guarantee that He will not become the devil tomorrow?
5. Can a mutable God be trusted?

FOURTEEN

THE OMNIPRESENCE OF GOD

*I*t may come as a surprise to some that this attribute of God needs defending. That God is everywhere present in the totality of His person is so basic to Christian thought that most Christians will be surprised to find that it too is being attacked today.

But this should not really surprise us. When processian thinkers deny what they call the "omni" attributes of God, they mean *all* the attributes of God from omniscience to omnipresence. They are forced to this path of apostasy by their commitment to rationalism.

Once God's nature is determined solely on the basis of what is "coherent" or "rational," then God's omnipresence must go the way of all the other "omni" attributes of God. After all, who can give a "coherent" explanation of "how" and "in what way" God can be everywhere without somehow becoming everything? Do God and the world occupy the same space and time? Then how do they differ?

Or, again, if God is finite and is "in" time like man, then the fastest He can go is the speed of light. Thus to go from one end of the universe to the other means that God cannot be everywhere at the same time. Thus Whitehead and his disciples claimed that God must struggle to overcome gravity and inertia.

The Bible, however, teaches the omnipresence of God in such passages as 1 Kings 8:27; Psalm 139, Isaiah 40, Jeremiah 23:24; Acts 17:24-28, and Ephesians 1:22-23.

The rationale of prayer is based on the omnipresence of God. We can pray anywhere because God is everywhere. But the finite gods of the heathen are not omnipresent. They are limited by space as well as by time. Thus when Elijah fought his "battle of the gods" on Mount Carmel, he mocked the pagans by reminding them that their god was not omnipresent.

> Call out with a loud voice, for he is a god; either he is occupied or gone aside, or is on a journey, or perhaps he is asleep and needs to awakened (1 Kings 18:27).

If God is not omnipresent, then He can hear our prayers only if He happens to be near us at that moment. Maybe we'll get "lucky" and choose the right moment when God is passing by. We shudder to think of all the consequences of denying the omnipresence of God.

The historic Christian view is that the God of Scripture is omnipresent in the sense that He is infinite in His presence, i.e., His existence has no limits. There is no "cutting off point" for God where we can say that He begins or ends. God does not end on the boundaries of the finite universe we live in. He is greater than the universe. It is a mere speck of dust to the Almighty.

God is also omnipresent in that all things derive their existence from Him. Thus the time-space universe exists "in" God (Acts 17:28). He is actually holding together all things (Colossians 1:17). Thus He is everywhere present (Psalm 139).

God and Anthropomorphic Language

When processians such as Clark Pinnock argue against the timelessness of God, they appeal to those passages in Scripture which speak of God in temporal terms.[1] They deny that they are anthropomorphic and claim that we must interpret these passages in a literal sense.

Genesis 11:1-9 is a classic example. Some processians argue that God was ignorant of what man was up to. So, He went down to take a quiet look. Isn't this proof that God does not know the future?

First, no *future* building projects are mentioned anywhere in the text. The story has to do with what man had *already* built. If we take it literally, then God has no knowledge of the *past* or the *present*.

Second, the passage speaks of God in spatial terms such as "coming down" or "going up." If the processians are to be consistent, then they must say God is limited by space as well as by time. This means that God is not omnipresent. But this is not acceptable to Christians.

But if they say that the spatial language is only "anthropomorphic" and that God is really "spaceless," then their sole "Biblical" argument against the timelessness of God is overthrown.

Most "evangelical" processians on this point are quite hypocritical. In private conversation they are willing to state their objections to God's omnipresence. But when we ask them to put it in writing so we can document what they are saying, they refuse to do so. They know that they would soon lose their teaching positions in evangelical institutions.

Conclusion

We can pray with confidence because the Almighty is not limited by space or time. He can answer prayer anywhere, at any time. His omnipresence means that He is everywhere present in the totality of all His infinite attributes. When we pray, we are not just touching a part of God, but we are encountering the infinite Person of the Sovereign Creator of the universe.

Questions for Discussion

1. Is God everywhere?
2. Does this mean that He is everything?
3. If God is not omnipresent, what happens to prayer?
4. What is anthropomorphic language?

FIFTEEN

THE OMNISCIENCE OF GOD

T he doctrine of the omniscience of God comes naturally after God's omnipresence. If God is everywhere and is holding all things together by His power, then He knows everything about everything. His understanding is as limitless as His being.

Now this is so fundamental to the average Christian that it is hard for us to believe that some people who claim to be "evangelicals" deny the omniscience of God.

Perhaps part of the confusion is caused by their use of the old Socinian trick of redefining the word "omniscience" to mean the exact opposite of what orthodox theology has always meant by the term. Much of processian and moral government theology is nothing more than a classic example of "Humpty Dumpty-ism," in which orthodox terms are given heretical definitions in order to keep up the facade of being "Christian" as long as possible.

The Controversy in History

Jonathan Edwards, the father of the Great Awakening, faced a revival of Socinian theology in his own day that denied the foreknowledge of God. In his refutation of the idea that God cannot know the future, he began with this apology.

One would think it wholly needless to enter on such an argument with any that profess themselves Christians: but so it is; God's certain Foreknowledge of the free acts of moral agents, is denied by some that pre-

tend to believe the Scriptures to be the Word of God; and especially
as of late. I therefore shall consider the evidence of such a prescience
in the Most High.[1]

After the dust had cleared on the debate in Edwards's day, the lines
were clearly drawn. Evangelical Christians believed in the foreknowledge
of God and those who denied it should leave the Christian Church and
join the Unitarians. Those who did leave are to be admired for their
honesty.

In eighteenth-century England, the famous theologian and hymn-
writer, Augustus Toplady, waded into the battle against those who denied the foreknowledge of God. He pointed out that while classic
Arminian theology teaches God's foreknowledge, in their haste to escape
Reformed theology, some Arminians had left their own faith and had
jumped into a form of atheism! Toplady stated:

> If you say, "God does not know what the event will be;" I give you
> up as incurable. It is less impious to deny the very existence of God,
> than to strip him of his omniscience and thereby make him (as far as
> in you lies) such an one as yourself. By pleading divine ignorance (I
> shudder at the very idea) you certainly slip out of my hands; and it
> is the only way by which you can. But your escape costs you very dear.
> In flying from Calvinism, you jump into atheism.[2]

Toplady demonstrates on pages 94, 107-08, 111, 154ff., 232, 274, and
756 that the denial of the foreknowledge of God is not in accord with
the Reformed doctrine of the Church of England or with the theology
of Wesleyan Arminianism. He labels such denials as heresy and atheism.

It was not until the Fundamentalist/Liberal debates at the beginning
of the twentieth century that the issues of God's infinite nature and foreknowledge surfaced once again. But this time the evangelical Christians
lost and the mainline denominations and their seminaries were taken
over by liberal theologians who taught that god was a finite being who
was not omniscient, omnipotent, sovereign, immutable, or perfect.

The Unitarians rightfully complained that most mainline theologians
were now "Unitarian" in everything but membership. They should therefore in all honesty leave the Christian Church and join with them. If
they did, the Unitarian Church would become one of the biggest denominations in the United States. But the cost in terms of money and
power prevented most liberals being honest enough to make the break.

The fall of the mainline denominations into the hands of the processians resulted in a mass exodus of those who truly loved the Christian faith. They went on to establish the fundamental and evangelical denominations that exist today. In some cases, as with Gresham Machen, the liberals actually forced conservative Christians to leave.

An Essential Attribute

Omniscience has always been viewed as an essential attribute of God in Christian theology. The conviction that God knows everything has always meant that He knows everything only as *God* can know it. Thus God's knowledge of everything must be defined in terms of God's *divine* nature.

Since all the attributes interrelate and define each other, this means that the *only* knowledge that God can have is an eternal, self-existent, infinite, and perfect knowledge. It does not matter if we are thinking of God's knowledge of Himself, the world, or the future. His knowledge can never be anything less than *divine* because He is GOD.

God's knowledge is as eternal as He is. What God knows now, He has always known, and will always know. We can never draw a line and say, "Here is where God's knowledge *began* because He first *learned* of it here." If God is eternal, then His knowledge has no beginning. Neither does it have an end, as if we could draw another line and say, "Here is where God's knowledge *ends*. He cannot know anything beyond this point."

Since God's knowledge is eternal, it is likewise self-existent and infinite. It is self-existent in that it is not dependent on anything, not even time. It is infinite in that His knowledge of Himself or of the universe has no limits. As the psalmist declared, "His understanding is *infinite*" (Psalm 147:5, emphasis mine).

God's knowledge is immediate and complete. It is not built up little by little each time the dice are thrown. In that it is eternal, infinite, and self-existent, it is no surprise to find the Bible saying that God is "*perfect* in knowledge" (Job 37:16, emphasis mine). Thus God's knowledge does not increase or decrease. It does not depend on the investigation of future events. He knows all things from all eternity. As Job declared, "He knows . . . and He sees . . . without investigating" (Job 11:11).

But what if we decide that God cannot know the future? We end up with a finite god who was ignorant of *all* things from *all* eternity! He did not know that he would create the world. He did not even know what he would create or what would happen to it. All his actions are strictly based on "spur of the moment" decisions and haphazard events. In short, having no foresight, this god was *blind*. Having no foreknowledge, this god was *ignorant*. Before the world was created, his mind was a dark void of emptiness. Is this god the GOD of the Bible?

Another thing to consider when thinking about the idea that God does not know the future is that this means that God cannot love people before they are born! Thus God did not love us before He made the world. Since God cannot know the free acts of men, particularly their sins, then He cannot know us as we are going to be. The implications are staggering! No one can say that Jesus loved him and died for him on the cross, because He did not know about him or his sins for they were yet future! Is this what the Bible teaches?

Biblical Passages

The Biblical support for the omniscience of God is so overwhelming that processians generally ignore the Bible and argue on the basis of their "reason" and "intuition." We prefer to argue from *God's* reason and intuition as revealed in Scripture.

In Acts 15, when James spoke at the Jerusalem Council on the inclusion of the Gentiles into the Church, he stated two things. First, the Old Testament prophets had foreknown and predicted that the Gentiles would come into the Church (vv. 15-17). Second, God knew from all eternity whatever He was going to do in space-time history.

> Known unto God are all His works from the beginning of the world (Acts 15:18, KJV).

God's omniscience means that God knows all of space-time history from the beginning to the end. How else can He know what He is going to do throughout time? G. V. Lechler comments,

> The meaning of the words which James adds, is the following: That which happens in our day, God knew from the beginning, and had resolved to perform; that which we live to see is simply the execution of an eternal decree of God.[3]

In his classic commentary on Acts, J. A. Alexander states,

. . . the reception of the Gentiles into the Church was no afterthought or innovation, but a part of the divine plan from the beginning . . . *from eternity*.[4]

The Lutheran scholar Lenski points out that the Greek literally reads, "known from the eon his work to God"! He comments further:

Far more preferable is the translation of the A.V., which is also well supported textually. . . . James quite pertinently declares that an eon before the time that God would do a work he already knew what that work would be and thus could foretell it. . . . God is now doing a work which he ages ago knew he would do.[5]

Heinrich Meyer also points out that:

By *whom* they were known from the beginning, is evident from the context, namely, by *God* who accomplishes them in the fulness of time. He accordingly carries into effect nothing which, has not been from the beginning evident to Him in His consciousness and counsel; how *important* and *sacred* must they consequently appear![6]

James declares that God knew all things from eternity. Before He created the world, He knew what He was going to create. He knew of the Fall of man into sin and guilt. It did not take the Almighty by surprise. But He also knew that He would send His Son to die on the cross for our sins (1 Peter 1:20; Revelation 13:8). Thus He preached the Gospel to a fallen Adam and Eve and told them of a coming Savior (Genesis 3:15).

The Gospel promises that a Savior would crush the head of the serpent and set us free from sin is proof of the foreknowledge of God. Salvation was not a hasty plan thrown together by God after He was surprised by Adam's sin. The Bible speaks of salvation as something that was known and planned by God *before* the space-time world was created. (See Ephesians 1:4; 3:11; 2 Timothy 1:9; Titus 1:2; 1 Peter 1:20; Revelation 13:8.)

Since all things are known to God from eternity, then He knows all things at any point of history. In Matthew 24:35, we are told that "*from the foundation of the world*" God has prepared a kingdom for the saints when Jesus comes back. The names of those who will enter that kingdom are known to God "*from the foundation of the world*" (Revelation

13:8; 17:8, emphasis mine).

That God would create something while not knowing what He was creating and what would happen to it is absurd. If an earthly king is deemed wise by Jesus in Luke 14:28-32 because he knows ahead what he is going to do, how much more the heavenly King of the universe! Hannah rejoiced because, "The Lord is a God of knowledge" (1 Samuel 2:3), not of ignorance.

In Psalm 139:1-6, the Psalmist claims that God knows everything about him *before* he opens his mouth. Jeremiah 32:19 declares that God's "eyes are open to all the ways of the sons of men." Hebrews 4:13 makes it clear that "all things are open and laid bare" before God. And 1 John 3:20 declares that God "knows all things." Can words be plainer?

The choice ultimately comes down to believing either those who say, "God does *not* know all things," or the Word of God, which says, "God knows *all* things."

Prayer and Omniscience

Does prayer inform God? Is He ignorant of our needs until we state them? Or does God already know what we need *before* we ask? Does He know what we will ask *before* we ask for it? Isaiah tells us:

> Before they call, I will answer; and while they are still speaking, I will hear (Isaiah 65:24).

The Lord Jesus taught His disciples,

> Your heavenly Father knows what you need, *before* you ask Him (Matthew 6:8, emphasis mine).

David even claimed that God knew what he was going to ask *before* he asked it!

> Even *before* there is a word on my tongue, behold, O Lord, *Thou dost know it all* (Psalm 139:4, emphasis mine).

The purpose of prayer is not to inform God of what we need as if He were ignorant. No, the purpose of prayer is to deepen our trust and confidence in God. Prayer reminds us of the promises and provisions of God. It enables us to become mighty in faith.

Now the processians will complain that since God already knows what we need before we ask and knows ahead of time what we shall ask before we ask it, then prayer is useless. This is a perfect example of the stupidity of following "reason" instead of obeying revelation!

Christians delight in the fact that God knows what they need not only *all the time* but *from all eternity*. They rejoice that God will answer in accordance with *His* will, not theirs, because they assume that God knows what is best for them (Matthew 6:10; 1 John 5:14).

Do We Know More Than God?

We must also object to the argument put forth by some processians that God is not omniscient because He cannot know by experience what man knows. For example, God cannot know how watermelon or any other food tastes because He has no tastebuds! Since God does not know all that man knows then man actually has greater knowledge than God!

The psalmist did not hesitate to call such ideas "senseless" and "stupid."

> Pay heed, you senseless among the people;
> And when will you understand, stupid ones?
> He who planted the ear, does He not hear?
> He who formed the eye, does He not see (Psalm 94:8-9)?

God does not need an ear to hear, an eye to see, a tongue to taste, a nose to smell, or a finger to touch. Who do you think created all the sights, sounds, smells, colors, and textures? He who created the watermelon knows *more* about it than man, not less.

He who made this world, and made it beautiful with colors of every hue, with billions of brilliant flowers that fill the air with sweet perfume, with the songs of innumerable birds, and with the softness of a newborn baby, is not jealous of the poor, pathetic, five senses of man. God's perception and experience of the world He has made is beyond our comprehension to even express. It is too high! It is too wonderful!

God's Foreknowledge of the Future

Now that we have looked at God's omniscience in general, we need to establish that this omniscience extends to the future. By the "future," we include all the details of everything that will happen, including the free acts of men and angels. The following arguments establish this Biblical position.

The Plain Statement of Scripture

For those who are satisfied by the plain statement of Scripture, the following passages are all that are needed.

- God "foreknows" the future: Acts 2:23; Romans 8:29; 11:2; 1 Peter 1:2
- God "foresees" the future: Galatians 3:8

To these we add God's foreordination and predestination, because it is impossible to foreordain something unless you know about it.

- God "foreordains" the future: 1 Peter 1:20
- God "predestines" the future: Romans 8:29, 30; Ephesians 1:5, 11

Foreknowledge: The Chief Attribute of God

The prophet Isaiah viewed God's infallible and perfect knowledge of the future as the final proof of Jehovah's divinity. The gods of the heathen could not tell the future. But the God of Israel could foresee and foretell it in the greatest detail.

God begins with a challenge to the gods of heathendom.

"Present your case," the Lord says.
"Bring forward your strong arguments,"
the King of Jacob says (Isaiah 41:21).

Now we will see who is GOD! He is GOD who knows all things including the future and can *prove* that He knows the future by infallibly foretelling it.

Let them bring forth and declare to us
    what is going to take place; . . .
Or announce to us *what is coming.*
Declare the things *that are going to come afterward,*

That we may know that you are gods (Isaiah 41:22-23, emphasis mine).

When the pagan gods fail the test, God mocks them.

> Behold, you are of no account,
> And your work amounts to nothing.
> He who chooses you is an abomination (Isaiah 41:24).

Then God sets forth His case for divinity.

> I have aroused one from the north, . . .
> And *he will come* upon rulers as upon mortar,
> Even as the potter treads clay.
> Who has declared this *from the beginning*, that we might know?
> Or, *from former times*, that we may say, "He is right!"
>   (Isaiah 41:25-26, emphasis mine).

> There is no God besides Me.
> And who is like me? Let him proclaim and declare it; . . .
> And let them declare to them the things that *are coming*
> And the events that are going to take place
>   (Isaiah 44:6, 7, 26, 28, emphasis mine).

> Ask Me about the *things to come* concerning My sons. . . .
> Who has announced this *from of old?*
> Who has *long since declared it?*
> Is it not I, the LORD?
> And there is no other God besides Me
>   (Isaiah 45:11, 21, emphasis mine).

> I am God, and there is no one like Me,
> Declaring *the end from the beginning*
> And *from ancient times* things which have been done. . . .
> Truly I have spoken; truly I will *bring it to pass.*
> I have planned it, surely I will do it
>   (Isaiah 46:9-11, emphasis mine).

God's whole case for His deity rests on the certainty of His perfect knowledge of the future in all of its details. This is why Christian theology has always stated that any god that does not know or control the future is no God at all! The processians and moral government theologians are attacking the Godhood of God when they deny His foreknowledge.

The End from the Beginning. Notice that in Isaiah 46:10, God declares that He knows "the end from the beginning." The arrangement of the words is striking because it is the exact opposite of the way *man* knows history.

Because man is limited by space-time, he must always learn about things as they unfold in time, i.e., from the beginning to the end. The "end" is not known to us. We must gradually work our way toward the end. Thus human knowledge is gradual and accumulative. It is always from "the beginning to the end."

But God tells us that He knows the end *before* the beginning. Thus when the world began, He already knew all of history "from the end to the beginning." Thus His knowledge is not gradual or cumulative like man's. It is eternal, infinite, perfect, and *timeless.*

Many Examples of God's Foreknowledge

All that is needed to refute the Socinian idea that God does not know the future acts of men is to find just *one* passage which plainly states that God foreknew what a certain man would do before he did it. If just *one* free act of man is foreknown and the man is still held accountable for that act, then *all* the acts of men can be foreknown without affecting human accountability in any sense.

In *hundreds* of Biblical passages God foreknows what people were going to do before they existed, were born, grew up, or thought or planned about doing anything. But we will limit ourselves to just a few sample passages.

Abraham, the Exodus, and Foreknowledge. God told Abraham that his descendants would become slaves in Egypt for four hundred years, but after that God would liberate them. And God said to Abraham:

> Know for certain that your descendants will be strangers in a land that is not theirs, where they will be enslaved and oppressed four hundred years. But I will also judge the nation whom they will serve; and afterward they will come out with many possessions (Genesis 15:13-14).

The passage is remarkable for several reasons. First, it refutes the claims of those who say that Biblical prophecies are not "certain," i.e., infallible. Notice that God says what He foreknows and foretells will happen "*for certain.*"

Second, the certainty of God's foreknowledge refutes the processian idea that "chance" controls the future. God determines the future according to this passage.

Third, notice clearly that although the future oppression of the Jews at the hands of the Egyptians is declared to be *certain* because it is *foreknown* and *foretold* by God, this did not negate the *accountability* of the Egyptians. Thus God will judge them for their sins. This at once forever refutes the argument that if God has an infallible and perfect knowledge of the future, this means that man is not accountable for his acts. Were the rebellious attitudes and actions of Pharaoh in refusing to let the Jews go foreknown and foretold by God (Exodus 3:19; 7:14; 9:30; 11:9)? Yet, he was still held accountable to his Maker.

Foreknowledge of Future Acts. The free acts of a king yet to be born three hundred years in the future were foreknown and predicted in 1 Kings 13:1-6. Let processians here note that prophecies are infallible, "the thing shall *surely* come to pass" (v. 32).

The future acts of Ahab (1 Kings 21:20-22), Hazael (2 Kings 8:12), Cyrus (Isaiah 44:28) were foreknown and foretold by God. Daniel even foretold the future empires of the world: Babylonian, Medo-Persian, Greek, and Roman.

The Messianic Prophecies. Perhaps the greatest proofs of the foreknowledge of God are the hundreds of Messianic prophecies in which God reveals in minute detail what Jesus and those around Him will do in the future. The signs and place of His birth, the slaughter of the infants, His flight into Egypt, the coming of John the Baptist, the cleansing of the Temple, the triumphant entry on an ass, the betrayal by Judas, the plucking of the beard, the death on the cross, and the empty tomb, all bear eloquent witness to the omniscient eye of the Almighty.

The Foreknowledge of Jesus. As incarnate Deity, Jesus knew and predicted the future free acts of men. He knew that Judas would betray Him from the very beginning (John 6:64). He knew all the details of Peter's life, including his denial in the courtyard, his repentance, ministry, old age, and final death (Mark 14:30; John 21:18, 19). He described in great detail how the Temple and Jerusalem would be destroyed some thirty-seven years before it took place (Matthew 24:2)

Human History is His-story. Just as Genesis tells of the beginning of human history, the Book of Revelation tells us how it will end in terms of being His-story. He is the Lord of History, and nations rise and fall under His decrees. History is traveling along a predetermined path toward a predetermined victory over evil.

Prophecy Impossible Without Foreknowledge

The reliability of Biblical prophecy is based on the fact that God is said to tell us what He *knows* will happen in the future. Thus God told Jeremiah that He knew all about him before he was even born (Jeremiah 1:5). When God promised Abraham that he would become the father of many nations, He was "calling those things which are not [yet] as though they were" (Romans 4:17).

Biblical prophecy is never presented as "guesswork" or "a shot in the dark" on God's part as if its future fulfillment depended on the "roll of the dice." The prophets declare what *will* infallibly come to pass.

No Passages to the Contrary

Do any passages clearly state that God is *not* all-knowing? No! Do any passages state in clear language that God is ignorant of the future? No! Do any passages teach that God is ignorant by nature? No! Are there any passages which teach that foreknowledge is impossible? No!

Then what do "evangelical" processians do when they want to give a Biblical argument against God's foreknowledge of the future? They argue that several Biblical passages suggest that God learned something *new* that He did not know beforehand.

"Didn't God *ask* Adam where he was? Doesn't this mean He did *not* know where Adam was hiding? Didn't God have to investigate the Tower of Babel to learn what man was doing? Didn't God learn something new about Abraham when he was willing to kill his son?" Such arguments are the typical "Biblical" evidences given by processians to prove that God cannot know the future. But in every case the passage concerns God's *present* knowledge of man and actually has nothing to do with the future.

When God called out to Adam, "Where are you?", He was asking the *present* whereabouts of (Genesis 3:9). It had nothing to do with the future. He did not say, "Where will you be tomorrow?" If the processian argument were valid, then God would not know the *present location of anyone* It doesn't take much to see the absurdity of that line of reasoning.

The same can be said of Genesis 11, where God "came down" to see what man was doing. The knowledge that God sought had nothing to do with the future. If we take this passage literally, then God does not have any *present* knowledge of what people are doing.

When the angel told Abraham on the mountain where Isaac was almost sacrificed that, "now I know that you fear God," he was referring to the *present spiritual* condition of Abraham's heart. The issue has nothing to do with future events. It concerns the attitude of Abraham's heart. If this passage is to be taken literally, then what do we do with the dozens of passages that plainly teach that God knows the hearts of all men (Jeremiah 17:10; Hebrews 4:12-13)?

Christian theologians have always interpreted the above passages as being anthropomorphic in nature, i.e., God is described in human terms in a figurative way. Thus whenever the Bible talks about God's going from place to place, looking at this or that, having hands, eyes, or ears, none of these should be taken literally any more than when God is described as having the wings of a bird! Thus Adam was asked the question for *his* benefit, not God's. It was *Abraham* who needed to know the condition of his heart, not God.

In terms of hermeneutics, if we must choose between a didactic passage in Scripture where God's foreknowledge is clearly taught and a historical narrative where figurative language is used, the didactic passages must be given the dominance.

Conclusion

The Scriptures clearly teach that God as GOD knows all things. This means His understanding of Himself is perfect and complete. He knows all about the past, present, and future of the universe which He made out of nothing. And He knows about everything and everyone in it. Nothing is hidden from the eyes of Him with whom we have to do.

Questions for Discussion

1. What religious group redefined the word "omniscience" to mean the opposite of what it originally meant?
2. What great Christian leaders have spoken out against those who limit the knowledge of God?
3. Is omniscience an essential attribute of God?
4. What does the Bible teach on this subject?
5. Do we know more than God?

SIXTEEN

THE OMNIPOTENCE
OF GOD

This is one of the most misunderstood and the most maligned attributes of God. Yet, it is an essential attribute that makes God GOD. Perhaps the best way to start our study of this attribute is to point out what we do *not* mean when we say that God is omnipotent.

The attribute of omnipotence does not mean that God has absolute freedom to do or be anything at all even if it contradicts His nature. While God is free to be GOD in all the fullness of His divine nature, He is not free to become non-God or act in a manner inconsistent with His immutable, perfect, good, and holy nature.

This at once dismisses one Greek riddle which freshman philosophy students love to discuss: Can God make a rock so big He can't move it? Now, in order for this riddle to work it must be assumed that God can do absolutely *anything* in the Greek sense of an open-ended chance-based universe. Once this assumption is granted, the riddle takes on the character of a complicated question in logic which means that more than one question is being asked at the same time.

The first question is, Can God do *absolutely* anything He wants?

The second question assumes the first question was answered in the affirmative: Well, if God can do *anything*, then can He do something which is non-Godlike? Can God contradict Himself by making something more powerful and Godlike than Himself? Namely, can He make a rock which is *more* powerful than Himself? If not, then God cannot do absolutely anything. But if so, then He is not all-powerful.

Those who hold to an "open" view of God, such as Rice, have no answer to the riddle. But orthodox Christians do. We disagree with the first basic assumption because Scripture states that God "*cannot* deny Himself" (2 Timothy 2:13, emphasis mine). Thus God cannot lie or do anything that is inconsistent with His divine nature.

The Meaning of Omnipotence

Omnipotence means that God is an infinite Power who can never be depleted, drained, or exhausted. He is infinitely perfect in that He is limitless, eternal, and self-existent. God does not need to draw on any source of power outside Himself for anything.

Thus the omnipotence of God speaks of the infinite reservoir of power resident within God, at His disposal whenever He cares to exercise it in accordance with His nature.

It is in this sense that God is given the name the "Almighty" or "All-Powerful One" in Scripture no fewer than fifty-six times! God is called the "Almighty" in the Law, the Writings, and the Prophets. From the book of Genesis to the book of Revelation, God reveals Himself as the Omnipotent God.

Since the only limitations to omnipotence are those that arise out of the nature of God, once God sets out to do something, nothing and no one outside of Himself can defeat Him. Thus nothing that does not contradict His nature is *impossible* for God to do. Nothing outside Him can limit His power. (See Genesis 18:14; Job 42:2; Psalm 115:3; Jeremiah 32:17, 27; Daniel 4:35; Zechariah 8:6; Matthew 19:26; Luke 1:37.)

Has anyone shown how and in what way the nature of God prevents His knowing the future? No! Is knowing the future too difficult for God? Of course not! Time is only an aspect of the world which He made. No one has ever shown how God's *nature* is contradicted by His knowledge of the future.

The omnipotence of God is essential for all the other attributes of God. If He is not omnipotent, how can He be self-existent? If His power is anything less than infinite, then how can it be eternal? How can God be omnipresent or omniscient if He is not the Almighty? How can He be the Creator and Sustainer of all things unless His power knows no beginning or end?

Divine Sovereignty or Providence

It may come as a surprise to some evangelicals but God's sovereignty or providence has always been viewed as one of the attributes of God by the Christian Church. It follows naturally from and is based upon God's omnipotence. Indeed, as we shall see, it was viewed as an essential attribute of God by the early Church and anyone who dared to deny it was called an atheist. Divine providence was thus not viewed as something that God could jettison and still remain GOD. It is an essential part of historic Christian theism.

Divine sovereignty means that God is in control of this universe and that there is no such thing as chance or luck. Everything has a divine purpose and fits in with God's plan of the ages which we call "history" or "His-story." It means that He is the King of kings and the Lord of lords and that nothing happens in this world but must first pass through His will.

Since God is the Creator of all things, He has the moral right to do whatever He wants with what He has made. This is Paul's argument in Romans 9. God is the Potter and we are the clay. Thus He can do with us as He pleases.

When someone asks us, "Do you believe in free will?" we usually reply, "Yes, God has a free will and He can do with you as He pleases." This usually provokes the rather frantic response, "I don't mean God's free will. I mean *man's* free will!"

This highlights the main problem that afflicts most discussions of God's sovereignty and man's will. The humanist will always begin with *man* and will strive to establish that *man's will* is ultimate in a universe ruled by chance, while theists will begin with *God* and will strive to establish that *God's will* is ultimate in His creation.

We believe with the Apostle Paul that if the choice comes down to either exalting God or man, God is to be given the preeminence in all things (Romans 3:4).

Should We Begin with Man or with God?

Where should we begin when studying God's sovereignty and man's responsibility? Should we begin with man and establish his free will and then define divine sovereignty in such a way that it does not conflict with man? Or, should we begin with God and His free will and then develop our understanding of man from that viewpoint?

For Bible-believing Christians, only one answer is possible. We must begin where Scripture begins. And when we open the Bible, what do we find? The Bible begins with GOD, not man!

This forever establishes that we must begin with GOD and not man. Since GOD is the "measure of all things" and the Origin of meaning, man and his will have no meaning unless we first begin with God. Thus before we can understand what man is, we must first understand what God is.

If Genesis 1:1 teaches us anything, it teaches us that God is sovereign because He created what He wanted, when He wanted, and where He wanted. In His act of creation He was absolutely unlimited by anything other than His own nature. He was and remains sovereign over all that He has made. It is by His sovereign power that the universe is now being held together (Colossians 1:17). Everything is being worked together by God according to His sovereign will (Romans 8:28; Ephesians 1:11). Everything that happens, happens according to His free will (Romans 11:36).

The Scriptures always describe God as actively controlling and guiding the entire creation (Psalm 103:19). It is never viewed as bare potential. It does not matter if we consider such things as the wind, the rain, the grass, or the trees, God controls them all (Psalm 104:5-17). Even the brute beasts of the field gladly obey His sovereign will (Psalm 104:14-30).

But What About Man?

And what shall we say about mankind? Does God rule over the realm of mankiind? Both the Old and New Testaments clearly teach that God is the blessed Controller of all things including mankind (1 Samuel 2:3-10; Acts 17:26). As the book of Daniel declares, "The Most High is ruler over the realm of mankind" (Daniel 4:25, 34-37).

The only people pictured in the Bible as rebelling against God's sovereign control of all things are the wicked (Psalm 2:1-4; Daniel 4). As a matter of record, no one has ever found a single passage in Scripture which says that God is *not* sovereign, or in which one of the prophets or apostles rebelled against divine sovereignty as a false teaching. God's control over all things was viewed as a necessary truth by which the saints lived their daily lives (Job 42:2; James 4:13-15).

Does God's sovereignty mean that man is not accountable for his sin? No! Does this mean that man is a robot? No! Does this mean fatalism? No! It is actually the other way around. Because God is sovereign, He has the *right* to hold man responsible for his words and deeds. Because

God is sovereign, there *will* be a Day of Judgment. Because He is sovereign, He imposes His law on man regardless if man wants it, and will hold him responsible to keep it even when man rejects it!

Conclusion

We stand in amazement before the God who has revealed Himself in Scripture. He is infinitely perfect in all His being and power, and wondrous in all His mighty deeds. So all-powerful, all-wise, and all-knowing is the Lord of Glory! He is the great I AM, the Alpha and the Omega, the Beginning and the End.

Now unto The King eternal, immortal, invisible, the only wise God, be honor and glory forever and ever. Amen (1 Timothy 1:17).

Questions for Discussion

1. Can God make a rock so big that He cannot move it?
2. Can God do and be anything and everything?
3. In what ways is God limited by His own nature?
4. Was God tired after creating the universe?
5. What is Divine Sovereignty or Providence all about?

CONCLUSION

There is but one eternal triune God, existing in three persons: Father, Son, and Holy Spirit, who is infinite in all His attributes. He is everywhere present in the totality of His immutable person, being, perfection, power, knowledge, sovereignty, and glory. The earth is the Lord's and the fullness thereof, and they who live on it should bow before Him.

God's exalted nature cannot be compared or reduced to the finite gods of the heathen. They are mere idols, the works of men's hands or minds. They are no Gods at all, seeing they are limited in being, power, and knowledge. They are only creatures of space and time and cannot be the Creator of all things.

The Lord Jehovah sits on His throne and laughs at the puny attempts of men to make gods in their own limited and marred image. They are cracked cisterns that carry no water. They are trees without fruit and clouds without rain. Those who are deceived by them are not wise.

Who but the LORD of all the earth, all-knowing and all-powerful, is worthy of our wonder, awe, and praise? Who among the gods is like Him? He knows, He decrees, and He ordains the future destiny of men and angels. He is the master Potter and we are the clay.

Thus we worship and bow down before the Father of eternity. We lie prostrate in the dust before the God of the Prophets, Apostles, and the Fathers. We submit the eternal welfare of our immortal souls to Him who is the sovereign King of kings and Lord of lords. He alone is our God and the only God we will ever worship. To Him alone be all the glory!

END NOTES

CHAPTER 1: RELIGION, REASON, AND REVELATION

1. See B.B. Warfield, "On the Emotional Life of Our Lord," in Warfield, *The Person and Work of Christ* (Philadelphia: Presbyterian and Reformed, 1950), pp. 93-145.

CHAPTER 5: THE INCOMPREHENSIBILITY OF GOD

1. Stephen Davis, *Logic And The Nature Of God* (Grand Rapids, Mich.: Eerdmans, 1983), p. 19.
2. Ibid.
3. Ibid., p. 4.
4. Ibid., p. 16.

CHAPTER 9: INVISIBLE AND INCORPOREAL

1. David Basinger and Randall Basinger, eds., *Predestination and Free Will* (Downers Grove, Ill.: Inter Varsity Press, 1986), pp. 154-55.

CHAPTER 10: PERSONAL AND INFINITE

1. H. H. Leupold, *Exposition of the Psalms* (Grand Rapids, Mich.: Baker Book House, [1959] 1969), pp. 989-90.
2. Franz Delitzsch, *Biblical Commentary on the Psalms*, 3 vols., trans. Francis Bolton (Grand Rapids, Mich.: Eerdmans, n.d.) 3:400.

3. Carl Bernhard Moll, *The Psalms*, trans. with additions J. Fred. McCurdy; in John Peter Lange, ed., *Commentary on the Holy Scriptures*, Eng. ed. Philip Schaff, 24 vols. bound in 12 (Grand Rapids, Mich.: Zondervan [1872] 1976), vol. 9 (bound in vol. 5), pp. 671f.

CHAPTER 11: THE PERFECTION OF GOD

1. Franz Delitzsch, *Biblical Commentary on the Book of Job*, 2 vols., trans. Francis Bolton (Grand Rapids, Mich.: Eerdmans, n.d.) 2:301.

CHAPTER 12: THE ETERNITY OF GOD

1. Stephen T. Davis, *Logic and the Nature of God* (Grand Rapids, Mich.: Eerdmans, 1983), p. 11.
2. Ibid., p. 16.
3. Ibid., p. 11.
4. Ibid., p. 23.
5. Ibid., p. 22.
6. Ibid., p. 23.
7. Ibid., p. 24.

CHAPTER 13: THE IMMUTABILITY OF GOD

1. In David Basinger and Randall Basinger, ed., *Predestination and Free Will* (Downers Grove, Ill.: Inter Varsity Press, 1986), p. 155.
2. Ibid., p. 96.
3. Ibid., p. 154.
4. C. F. Keil and F. Delitzsch, *Biblical Commentary on the Pentateuch*, 3 vols., trans. James Martin (Grand Rapids, Mich.: Eerdmans, rep. 1968) 3:467.
5. Clark Pinnock, *Perspectives in Evangelical Theology* (n.p., n.d.), p. 40.
6. Charles H. Spurgeon, *The Treasury Of David*, 7 vols. (various editions), vol. 4 (1884), p. 426.
7. Cited in Ibid., p. 272.
8. Carl Bernhard Moll, *The Psalms*, trans. with additions J. Fred. McCurdy; in John Peter Lange, ed., *Commentary on the Holy Scriptures*, Eng. ed. Philip Schaff, 24 vols. bound in 12 (Grand Rapids, Mich.: Zondervan [1872] 1976), vol. 9 (bound in vol. 5), pp. 521f.
9. Joseph Addison Alexander, *The Psalms, Translated and Explained* (Grand Rapids, Mich.: Baker Book House, [1873] 1975), p. 413.
10. Franz Delitzsch, *Biblical Commentary On The Psalms*, 22 ed., trans. Franu's Bolton, 3 vols. (Grand Rapids, Mich.: Eerdmans, rep. 1968) 3:117.

11. Matthew Henry, *Commentary On The Whole Bible* (various editions [1710]), comments on Psalm 102:23-28.

12. Ibid., comments on Malachi 3:1-6.

13. Albert Barnes, *Notes On the Old Testament* (Grand Rapids, Mich.: Baker Book House, rep. 1960), vol. 16, p. 490.

14. C. F. Keil, *Biblical Commentary on the Twelve Minor Prophets*, trans. James Martin, 2 vols. (Grand Rapids, Mich.: Eerdmans, rep. 1969) 2:462.

15. Thomas Moore, *Haggai And Malachi*, (London: Banner Of Truth, [1856] 1960), p. 157.

16. Joseph Mayor, *The Epistle Of James* (Grand Rapids, Mich.: Zondervan [1892]) p. 61.

CHAPTER 14: THE OMNIPRESENCE OF GOD

1. David Basinger and Randall Basinger, eds., *Predestination and Free Will* (Downers Grove, Ill.: Inter Varsity Press, 1986), p. 152.

CHAPTER 15: THE OMNISCIENCE OF GOD

1. The Works Of Jonathan Edwards, 2 vols. (Edinburgh: The Banner of Truth Trust, 1974), 1:30.

2. The Complete Works of Augustus Toplady (Harrisonburg, Va.: Sprinkle Pub., 1988), p. 756.

3. Gotthard V. Lechler, *The Acts of the Apostles*, trans. with additions Charles F. Schaeffer; in John Peter Lange, ed., *Commentary on the Holy Scriptures*, Eng. ed. Peter Schaff, 24 vols. bound in 12 (Grand Rapids, Mich.: Zondervan [1866] 1976), vol. 18 (bound in vol. 9), pp. 280-81.

4. J. A. Alexander, *Commentary on the Acts of the Apostles* (Grand Rapids, Mich.: Zondervan, 1956), pp. 545-46.

5. R. C. H. Lenski, *The Acts of the Apostles* (Minneapolis, Minn.: Augsburg Pub. House, [1934] 1961), pp. 611-12.

6. Heinrich A. W. Meyer, *Critical and Exegetical Handbook to the Acts of the Apostles*, 4th. ed., trans. Paton J. Gloag, rev. William P. Dickson. *Meyer's Commentary on the New Testament* 4 (Winona Lake, Ind.: Alpha Publications [1884] 1979), p. 288.

CHAPTER 16: THE OMNIPOTENCE OF GOD

1. J. B. Lightfoot, trans. and ed., *The Apostolic Fathers: Clement, Ignatius, and Polycarp*, 2 parts in 5 vols. (Grand Rapids, Mich.: Baker Book House, [1889] 1981), part 1, vol. 2, p. 170.

2. Ibid., part 2, vol. 2, p. 572.
3. Ibid, p. 343.
4. Ibid., part 2, vol. 3, p. 87.
5. Ibid., part 2, vol. 1, p. 181.
6. The Patristic references to Greek philosophy are as follows: ANF 1: 28, 196-98, 272, 273-78, 331, 399, 401, 415; ANF 2: 75-76, 95-97, 111, 132; ANF 4: 50, 51, 130, 246, 272, 309.

SELECT BIBLIOGRAPHY

Achtemeir, Elizabeth. *The Feminine Crisis in the Christian Faith.* New York: Abingdon Press, 1965.

Adler, Mortimer J. *How to Think About God.* New York: Macmillan Pub. Co., 1980.

Alexander, Samuel. *Space, Time, and Deity.* London: Macmillan and Co., 1927.

Archer, Gleason L. *Encyclopedia of Bible Difficulties.* Grand Rapids, Mich.: Zondervan Pub., 1982.

Archer, William. *God and Mr. Wells.* New York: Alfred A. Knopf, 1917.

Baker's Dictionary of Theology. Edited by Everett F. Harrison. Grand Rapids, Mich.: Baker Book House, 1960.

Baker, Rannie Belle. *The Concept of a Limited God.* Washington, D.C.: Shenandoah Pub. House, 1934.

Basinger, David, and Randall Basinger, eds. *Predestination and Freewill.* Downers Grove, Ill.: Inter Varsity Press, 1986.

Bavinck, Herman. *The Doctrine of God.* Edinburgh: Banner of Truth Trust, 1977.

Berkhof, Louis. *Systematic Theology.* London: Banner of Truth Trust, 1966.

Beunke, Donna A. *Religious Issues in Nineteenth-century Feminism*. Troy, N.Y.: The Whitston Pub. Co., 1982.

Bloesch, Donald G. *Is the Bible Sexist?* Westchester, Ill.: Crossway Books, 1982.

Binns, Leonard Elliott. *Mr. Wells's Invisible King*. London: S.P.C.K., 1919.

Boyce, James. *Abstract of Systematic Theology*. Christian Gospel Foundation, n.d.

Bradley, Francis Herbert. *Collected Essays*. New York: Books For Libraries Press, 1968.

Brightman, Edgar Sheffield. *A Philosophy of Religion*. New York: Prentice Hall, Inc., 1940.

_____. *The Problem of God*. Nashville: Abingdon Press, 1930.

_____. *Creative Evolution*. New York: The Modern Library, 1944.

Bergson, Henri. *The Two Sources of Morality and Religion*. New York: Doubleday & Co., 1954.

Bulfinch, Thomas. *Myths of Greece and Rome*. New York: Penguin Books, 1981.

Carmody, Denise Lardner. *Feminism and Christianity*. Nashville: Abingdon Press, 1982.

Carson, Donald A. *Divine Sovereignty and Human Responsibility*. Atlanta: John Knox Press, 1981.

Charnock, Stephen, *The Existence and Attributes of God*. Sovereign Grace Book Club, 1958.

Clark, Gordon H. *John Dewey*. Philadelphia: Presbyterian & Reformed Pub. Co., 1960.

_____. *Religion, Reason, and Revelation*. Nutley, N.J.: The Craig Press.

_____. *William James*. Philadelphia: Presbyterian & Reformed Pub. Co., 1963.

Copleston, Frederick. *Contemporary Philosophy*. Westminster, Md.: The Newman Press, 1966.

Cranford, Alexander H. *The Religion of H.G. Wells and Other Essays*. London: T. Fisher Unwin, 1909.

Cumbey, Constance, *The Hidden Dangers of the Rainbow*. Shreveport, La.: Huntingdon House, 1983.

Cunningham, William. *Historical Theology*. London: Banner of Truth Trust, 1969.

Dabney, Robert L. *Lectures in Systematic Theology*. Grand Rapids, Mich.: Zondervan Pub., 1972.

Dagg, J.L. *Manual of Theology and Church Order*. Harrisonburg, Va.: Gano Books, 1982.

Danby, Herbert, ed. *The Mishnah*. Oxford: Oxford University Press, 1983.

Davis, Stephen T. *Logic and the Nature of God*. Grand Rapids, Mich.: Eerdmans, 1983.

Edwards, Jonathan. *The Works of Jonathan Edwards*. Edinburgh: Banner of Truth Trust, 1974.

Elseth, H. Roy. *Did God Know?* St. Paul, Minn.: Calvary United Church, 1977.

Epictetus. *Moral Discourses*. Thomas Gould, ed. New York: Washington Square Press, 1964.

Farrer, Austin. *Finite and Infinite*. London: Dacye Press, 1943.

Fiske, John. *The Idea of God as Affected by Modern Knowledge*. New York: Houghton, Mifflin, and Co., 1886.

Freeman, David H. *Tillich*. Philadelphia: Presbyterian & Reformed Pub. Co., 1962.

Gomes, Alan. *Lead Us Not Into Temptation*. La Mirada, Calif.: Telion, 1986.

Grant, Robert M. *The Early Christian Doctrine of God*. Charlottesville, Va.: University of Virginia Press, 1966.

Griffin, David Ray. *God, Power, and Evil: A Process Theodicy.* Philadelphia: Westminster Press, 1976.

Gruenler, Royce Gordon. *The Inexhaustible God: Biblical Faith and the Challenge of Process Theism.* Grand Rapids, Mich.: Baker Book House, 1983.

Gunton, Colin E. *Becoming and Being.* Oxford: Oxford University Press, 1978.

Hack, Roy Kenneth. *God in Greek Philosophy to the Time of Socrates.* Princeton, N.J.: Princeton University Press, 1966.

Hartshorne, Charles, and William L. Reese. *Philosophers Speak of God.* Chicago: University of Chicago Press, 1953.

Henry, Carl F.H. *Christian Faith and Modern Theology.* New York: Channel Press, 1964.

_____. *God, Revelation, and Authority.* Waco: Word, Inc., 1976.

Hodge, Charles. *Systematic Theology.* London: James Clarke & Co., 1960.

Harsberger, Caroline Thomas. *Gods and Heroes: A Quick Guide to the Occupations, Associations, and Experiences of the Greek and Roman Gods and Heroes.* Troy, N.Y.: The Whitson Pub. Co., 1977.

Jaeger, William. *The Theology of the Early Greek Philosophers.* Oxford: Oxford University Press, 1947.

James, William. *The Will to Believe.* New York: Dover Pub., n.d.

_____. *Essays in Radical Empiricism and a Pluralistic Universe.* Gloucester, Mass.: Peter Smith, 1967.

Johnson, Carlsten. *Day of Destiny.* Loma Linda, Calif.: The Untold Story Pub., 1982.

Kenny, Anthony. *The God of the Philosophers.* Oxford: Clarendon Press, 1979.

Latourette, Kenneth Scott. *A History of Christianity.* New York: Harper & Row, 1953.

Lightfoot, J.B. *The Apostolic Fathers*. Grand Rapids, Mich.: Baker Book House, 1981.

Machen, J. Gresham. *Christianity and Liberalism*. Grand Rapids, Mich.: Eerdmans, 1974.

Marsh, John. *The Fulness of Time*. London: Nisbet & Co., 1952.

Mill, John Stuart. *Three Essays on Religion*. New York: Greenwood Press, Pub., 1969.

Murray, John Courtney. *The Problem of God*. New Haven, Conn.: Yale University Press, 1964.

Nash, Ronald H. *The Concept of God*. Grand Rapids, Mich.: Zondervan Pub., 1983.

Ogletree, Thomas W. *The Death of God Controversy*. Nashville : Abingdon Press, 1966.

Olson, Carl, ed. *The Book of the Goddess Past and Present*. New York: Crossroads, 1983.

Olson, Gordon C. *Sharing Your Faith*. Chicago: Bible Research Fellowship, 1976.

On Process Theology. Grand Rapids, Mich.: Baker Book House, 1988.

Owen, John. *The Works of John Owen*. London: Banner of Truth Trust, 1966.

Pike, Nelson. *God and Timelessness*. New York: Schocken Books, 1970.

Pink, Arthur W. *The Attributes of God*. Grand Rapids, Mich.: Baker Book House, n.d.

Prestige, G.L. *God in Patristic Thought*. London: S.P.C.K., 1959.

Pringle-Pattison, A. Seth. *The Idea of God in the Light of Present Philosophy*. London: Clarendon Press, 1917.

Rice, Richard. *The Openness of God*. Nashville: Review & Herald Pub., 1979.

_____. *God's Foreknowledge and Man's Free Will.* Minneapolis, Minn.: Bethany House, 1985.

Schaeffer, Francis. *How Should We Then Live?* Old Tappan, N.J.: Fleming Revell Co., 1976.

Schaff, Philip. *The Creeds of Christendom.* Grand Rapids, Mich.: Baker Book House, 1983.

Sproul, R.C. *Chosen by God.* Wheaton, Ill.: Tyndale House Pub., 1986.

Steuer, Axel D., and McClendon, James William, Jr., eds. *Is God GOD?* Nashville: Abingdon Press, 1981.

Storms, C. Samuel. *The Grandeur of God.* Grand Rapids, Mich.: Baker Book House, 1984.

Strong, Augustus H. *Systematic Theology.* Valley Forge, Pa.: Judson Press, 1976.

Swinburne, Richard. *The Existence of God.* Oxford: Clarendon Press, 1979.

The History of the Christian Church. Grand Rapids, Mich.: Wm. B. Eerdmans, 1972.

The Truth Shall Make You Free. Chicago: Bible Research Fellowship, 1980.

Thomas, J.M. Lloyd. *The Veiled Being: A Comment on Mr. H.G. Wells' "God the Invisible King."* Birmingham: Cornish Brothers, Ltd., 1917.

Wells, H.G. *God the Invisible King.* New York: Macmillan & Co., 1917.

Whitehead, Alfred North. *Dialogues of Alfred North Whitehead.* Boston: Little, Brown, & Co., 1954.

_____. *Process and Reality.* New York: Macmillan Pub., 1978.

Wolfson, Harry Austryn. *The Philosophy of the Church Fathers.* Cambridge, Mass.: Harvard University Press, 1904.

Zeller, Eduard. *Outlines of the History of Greek Philosophy.* New York: Meridian Books, 1967.